Complementary Views on Complementarity

This publication was made possible by the financial support of

Koninklijke Nederlandse Akademie van Wetenschappen (KNAW)
Nederlandse Organisatie voor Wetenschappelijk Onderzoek (NWO)
Task Force International Criminal Court of the
Ministry of Foreign Affairs of The Netherlands

COMPLEMENTARY VIEWS
ON COMPLEMENTARITY

Proceedings of the International Roundtable on the
Complementary Nature of the International Criminal Court
Amsterdam, 25/26 June 2004

Edited by

Jann K. Kleffner
Gerben Kor

T·M·C·ASSER PRESS
The Hague

Published by T·M·C·Asser press
P.O.Box 16163, 2500 BD The Hague, The Netherlands

<www.asserpress.nl>

T·M·C·Asser press' English language books are distributed exclusively by:

Cambridge University Press, The Edinburgh Building, Shaftesbury Road,
Cambridge CB2 2RU, UK,
or
for customers in the USA, Canada and Mexico:
Cambridge University Press, 100 Brook Hill Drive, West Nyack, NY 10994-2133, USA

<www.cambridge.org>

ISBN 10: 90-6704-218-8
ISBN 13: 978-90-6704-218-5

PRINTED IN THE NETHERLANDS

PREFACE

The complementary nature of the International Criminal Court (ICC) is one of the fundamental principles of the Rome Statute for the International Criminal Court. It is laid down in the Preamble and in Article 1 and further defined in the form of admissibility requirements set forth in Articles 17 to 20. The principle of complementarity is the parameter, which defines the relationship between States and the ICC. It denotes that cases are admissible before the ICC if a State remains wholly inactive or is 'unwilling'[1] or 'unable'[2] to investigate and prosecute genuinely cases of genocide, crimes against humanity and war crimes as defined in Articles 5-8 of the Rome Statute.

Through the principle of complementarity, the system of international criminal justice established by the Rome Statute creates a presumption in favour of the repression of ICC crimes on the *national* level. National criminal jurisdictions are endowed with the primary task to investigate and prosecute these crimes. In contrast to the 'primacy over national courts' of the two *ad hoc* tribunals for the former Yugoslavia (ICTY)[3] and Rwanda (ICTR)[4] as well as the Special Court for Sierra Leone (SCSL),[5] complementarity entails that States can bar the ICC from investigating and prosecuting cases, by adequately adjudicating them in their domestic jurisdiction. To that end, the Rome Statute sets forth the substance of complementarity[6] and the procedure for its application[7] in the form of a regime of admissibility.

Complementarity raises a myriad of questions, a discussion of which is widely held to stand central in understanding the ICC. What role does

---

[1] For a definition of 'unwillingness', see Art. 17(2).
[2] For a definition of 'inability', see Art. 17(3).
[3] Art. 9 ICTY Statute.
[4] Art. 8 ICTR Statute.
[5] Art. 8 SCSL Statute.
[6] Art. 17 and 20(3).
[7] Art. 18, 19 and 53(1)(b).

complementarity play in ascertaining States' consent to the Rome Statute? What is the relationship between complementarity and State sovereignty? What is the effect of complementarity on national repression of ICC crimes? What room, if any, does complementarity leave for non-criminal responses to ICC crimes, such as truth commissions and amnesties? How should complementarity be conceptualised in order to make the ICC a success? These are only a few of the questions, which, as often with crucial questions, have proven controversial. At the same time, a number of academics and practitioners are actively engaged in making sense of complementarity, not the least some Ph.D. researchers who address complementarity from various angles.

These developments have prompted the *Amsterdam Center for International Law* and the Department of Legal Philosophy at the Law Faculty of the Free University of Amsterdam to hold an international expert roundtable on the 'Complementarity Principle of the Rome Statute of the International Criminal Court' on 25 and 26 June 2004. The roundtable provided a forum for high-level exchange between Ph.D. researchers and a limited number of experts on the subject. As a framework for that exchange, five Ph.D. researchers presented papers, which were commented upon by an expert, before the floor was opened for discussion. The papers and comments form the basis of the present book.

The first chapter, by Frédéric Mégret, University of Toronto, explores the question why States would join the ICC from a theoretical angle and addresses what role complementarity fulfils in States' decision to become party to the Rome Statute. The second chapter by Gerben Kor, Free University of Amsterdam, addresses the fundamental relationship between State sovereignty and complementarity. The commentator on the first two chapters is Dr. Bardo Fassbender, Humboldt University Berlin.

The third chapter, by Jann K. Kleffner of the *Amsterdam Center for International Law*, conceptualises complementarity as a catalyst for compliance of States with their obligation to investigate and prosecute ICC crimes. The comments were provided by Dr. Federica Gioia, International Criminal Court.

Dr. Claudia Cárdenas, at the time at the Humboldt University Berlin, wrote the fourth chapter on the question whether and to what extent complementarity provides room to respond to ICC crimes by means of an amnesty or truth commission. Darryl Robinson from the International Criminal Court provided comments.

Last but not least, Rod Jensen, University of British Columbia, presents his chapter which concentrates on the word 'genuinely' in the definition of complementarity and assessed the ways in which an understanding of that word will have a bearing on the effective functioning of the ICC. His chapter is commented upon by Judge Bert Swart, ICTY.

The editors wish to thank in the first place all the authors in this book, all chairs of the various sessions and all participants who made the roundtable on complementarity a great success. In all organisational and practical matters surrounding the conference, which is more than we could fathom, the invaluable assistance of Helen Klann is gratefully acknowledged. For her excellent work of language-editing of the present book, we thank Susan Park. And last but not least, we would like to thank Professors Arend Soeteman, Bert Swart, André Nollkaemper and Erika de Wet for their support.

Amsterdam, October 2005   Jann K. KLEFFNER and Gerben KOR

SUMMARY OF CONTENTS

TABLE OF CONTENTS

ABBREVIATIONS

AJIL	American Journal of International Law
Crim	Criminal
Court	International Criminal Court
DRC	Democratic Republic of Congo
EJIL	European Journal of International Law
ELSA	European Law Students' Association
EU	European Union
Eur	European
European Court	European Court of Human Rights
GAOR	General Assembly Official Records
ICC	International Criminal Court
ICC Statute	Rome Statute of the International Criminal Court
ICJ	International Court of Justice
ILC	International Law Commission
ICQL	International and Comparative Law Quarterly
ICTR	International Criminal Tribunal for Rwanda
ICTY	International Criminal Tribunal for the former Yugoslavia
IGOs	Intergovernmental Organizations
ILSA	International Law Student Association
Intl	International
IR	International relations
J	Journal
L	Law
NGOs	Non-governmental organizations
OTP	Office of the Prosecutor

PCIJ	Permanent Court of International Justice
Rome Statute	Rome Statute of the International Criminal Court
Regulations	Regulations of the Court, ICC
Rules	Rules of Procedure and Evidence
SCSL	Special Court for Sierra Leone
Statute	Rome Statute of the International Criminal Court
UK	United Kingdom
UN	United Nations
UNDP	United Nations Development Programme
UNGA	United Nations General Assembly
UNHCR	Office of the United Nations High Commissioner for Refugees
Universal Declaration	Universal Declaration on Human Rights
UNSCOR	United Nations Security Council Official Records
UNTS	United Nations Treaty Series
US	United States
VCLT	Vienna Convention of the Law of Treaties
WTO	World Trade Organization

Chapter 1
WHY WOULD STATES WANT TO JOIN THE ICC?
A THEORETICAL EXPLORATION BASED ON THE LEGAL
NATURE OF COMPLEMENTARITY

Frédéric Mégret*

For all the enthusiasm about the International Criminal Court (ICC), one of the most enduring mysteries surrounding it is why States would want to join it, and in such droves. After all, not long ago it seemed as if even the adoption of the Rome Statute was improbable. Once the Statute had been adopted, it seemed that the number of ratifications required for adoption would ensure that the ICC would come into existence – if at all – only in the distant future.

Most importantly, there seemed to be some very good fundamental reasons to think that States would not want to join the ICC. To the extent one subscribes to even a minimally realist approach to international relations and the idea that States operate fundamentally as something like egoistic inter-maximizers, it is difficult a priori to see what national interest might be derived from joining the Court.[1] The ICC promises no immediate strategic, military or even economic advantage and would seem to entail some not insignificant potential costs, such as that of having a State's nationals hauled before an international tribunal bent on prosecuting them for behaviour most likely undertaken as part of a State policy. If explaining

---

* Assistant Professor, Faculty of Law, University of Toronto.

[1] One is reminded of the very similar question that Andrew Moravcsik raised in the context of international human rights protection mechanisms which of course bear at least a family resemblance to international criminal justice arrangements: 'There is a real theoretical puzzle here. Why would any government, democratic or dictatorial, favor establishing an effective independent international authority, the sole purpose of which is to constrain its domestic sovereignty in such an unprecedentedly and overtly nonmajoritarian manner?'. A. Moravcsik, 'The Origins of Human Rights Regimes: Democratic Delegation in Postwar Europe', 54 *Intl Organization* (2000), 217, 219.

J.K. Kleffner & G. Kor (eds.), Complementary Views on Complementarity
© 2006, T·M·C·ASSER PRESS, *The Hague, The Netherlands and the Authors*

why States would want to join international human rights treaties 'where external enforcement tends to be minimal or non-existent'[2] is already difficult, then it seems that it would be even more so for an institution which, by the looks of it, will have substantially more enforcement power.

Needless to say, by the same token it seems crucial for the ICC's success as an institution that it be able to encourage as many States as possible to become party to the Rome Statute. The ICC is, and has always been, promoted as an institution whose fundamental objective is to become universal. An ICC without States Parties would be non-existent; an ICC with few and marginal States Parties would be irrelevant. Only a healthily global Court would seem to make sense of the ambition vested in the project of international criminal justice. There certainly does not seem much point in a Court that is merely a club of States that are otherwise already largely committed to the fight against impunity.

In fact, although this question is systematically shunned or simplified, there seems to be no question more central and in more urgent need of answering than the following: Why would a State want to take the risk that its nationals, particularly those acting in an official capacity, will be tried before an international tribunal?

Notwithstanding this implausibility, the ratification rate has progressed at breathtaking speed with the Court starting to work a mere four years after the signing of its Statute. Of course, the fact that many States have not joined the ICC should moderate the enthusiasm for international criminal justice. But, although the Court may yet turn out to be a total failure, the mere fact of its activity is often presented as being, in itself, an important signal that some things may be changing. How can one explain that paradox? Is it really one? How does it shed light on the nature of the ICC or perhaps on the development of the international order itself? Is it that the realist assumptions need to be corrected or that the ICC is and can be only less than what its supporters claim it to be?

This essay will try to make sense of these questions by asking how a universal ICC (or as universal an ICC as is achievable at any one time) might come about. International lawyers are typically less interested about *why* States join treaties and international institutions than they are about the

---

[2] O.A. Hathaway, 'The Cost of Commitment', 55 *Stanford L Rev* (2003), 1821, 1834.

fact *that* States join treaties and international institutions.[3] As Oona Hathaway has remarked in the context of international human rights, 'despite the proliferation of treaties and the growing attention to countries' decisions to join them, little attention has been paid to what influences countries' decisions to join these treaties.'[4] It has taken the renewal of interest in interdisciplinary research pioneered in the United States (US) in the last ten years for some of these central questions to begin to be taken seriously.[5] A fruitful agenda for research has thus been opened, provided it can be investigated rigorously and non-ideologically.

Note however that, even with the most positivist approach, exploring why States join the ICC should hardly be uninteresting: the validity and strength of States' reasons for joining the ICC will obviously be a key means of evaluating that institution's solidity and prospects.

In this chapter I do several, very different things, something that seems justified by the convoluted and contradictory nature of the problem. The presentation's starting-point and indeed main thrust is a minimally realist one, and I will seek to take that approach as far as I can reasonably do so. A quick word about the nature of my realism may be in order here. I say minimally realist because I do not want to assume that no State is capable of ever acting in a normative, inspired, even reasonably altruistic way, among other things, by joining the ICC. My realism is not of the unwavering, dogmatic kind. But, conversely, my impression is that international lawyers are too quick to take for granted that States join the ICC for the grand reasons for which they claim to join the ICC. I am deeply sceptical of a certain triumphalist international criminal law discourse which seems to assume that States should – or worse do – join the ICC just because such is the moral imperative of the times. What I want even less than being dogmatically realist, as will become apparent, is to assume uncritically that States behave spontaneously in ways designed to maximize the global common good.

---

[3] Hathaway points out that '[l]egal scholars … have tended to take it as a given that international treaties exist and that countries choose to join them', ibid. 1825 (footnote omitted), and that '[t]reaty ratification is … usually taken as the starting-point', ibid. 1829.

[4] Ibid. 1822 (footnote omitted).

[5] See, e.g., A.M. Slaughter, 'International Law and International Relations Theory: A Dual Agenda', 87 *AJIL* (1993), 205.

My realism, in other words, will be a methodological one. It is an ethics of scientific prudence that suggests that, confronted with a wild and improbable explanation of why a certain phenomenon occurs in the world and one that seems grounded in certain interests, one should have recourse to the former only if the latter proves inadequate. In fact, a good understanding of what realism does explain can also lead to a recognition of what it does not explain. It can, therefore, paradoxically reinforce the normative narrative by circumscribing the explanatory space where its comparative advantage is highest. Proceeding from the reality of State interest and then gradually trying to broaden one's frame of reference to explain the anomalies once they arise seems to me a healthier approach to the issue – one that is less at risk of mistaking its wishes for reality – than, for example, simply assuming that the international community is on an inevitable path to global integration and that States will follow suit sooner or later. At any rate, I think the ICC narrative would be reinforced if it could anchor an explanation of why States join the ICC into an explanation of why States would want to join the ICC.

More specifically, what I try to do is to come up with a convincing analysis of why States would want to join the Court, based on a computation of their national interest. I show that conventional explanations of the national interest do explain why some States might join the ICC, but unfortunately not those States that would matter most to the Court's success. I show that there comes a point when realism simply cannot offer a good explanation of why the States that do matter might have joined or might want to join the ICC (I do not actually offer evidence of whether any of these States actually have or are likely to join, although I believe that at least some have). This is where I depart from strict realism and try to introduce the idea that the national interest is in fact shaped by certain normative structures. I suggest that complementarity should be at the centre of any such theory. By that stage, it is difficult to escape the conclusion that joining the ICC for at least some of the less 'virtuous' States involves a substantially more significant normative effort than most brands of realism would allow.

Indeed, towards the end, it may seem to the reader as if I have moved widely away from my realist postulates. Perhaps I have. But the better explanation is that I have tried to show how a powerful and successful ICC *would* herald the rise of an international society which bears almost no relation to the one that we have known since Westphalia. However, although

I do not exclude the possibility of that change, I certainly do not make the claim that it has already happened.

Finally, note that this is not an empirical piece, nor does it claim to be. I am not making the empirical claim that States joining the ICC are actually joining the ICC for the reasons that are suggested. Rather, I am trying to come up with an internally consistent theory of why States would want to join the ICC if we took certain widespread premises about State behaviour as being minimally valid. It may be that no State will actually join the ICC for the reasons that the theory thinks it can predict. If that is the case, then some of the theory's premises will have been shown at least partially wrong, an interesting outcome in itself.

I am quite content with pursuing this purely theoretical course – a course in the end that is more concerned with our ideas about the ICC than with the ICC itself – because I think that theory matters and that in fact theory matters supremely when it comes to an institution that claims to challenge our understanding of international relations and is itself so loaded with ideological premises.[6] In fact, in good constructivist logic, I believe that theory matters because our ideas about international relations filter into the world in all kinds of ways. It makes a difference when approaching the issue of ratifying the ICC Statute if you think of yourself as a realist or an idealist – quite apart from the issue of whether either of these theories properly accounts for anything happening in the world. All theories are always to an extent self-realizing prophecies in the making.

I also believe, of course, that this theoretical pursuit is not incompatible with its empirical validation. In this presentation, because of time and space constraints, I only hint at widely available circumstantial evidence that seems relevant, but nothing prevents others more willing and able than I from trying to see how the theory stands up to the facts.

---

[6] See F. Mégret, 'Three Dangers for the International Criminal Court: A Critical Look at a Consensual Project', *Finnish Ybk of Intl L* (2002), 207.

1. A DETOUR THROUGH INTERNATIONAL RELATIONS THEORY
    AND SOME NOT TOTALLY SATISFACTORY EXPLANATIONS

Before we delve into the intricacies of the issues of complementarity, we need to take a detour through international relations to understand what exactly it is that I am trying to explain through complementarity.

Explaining why States would not want to join the ICC is the easy task; explaining why they would want to join the ICC is the hard one. Obviously, if no State had joined the ICC (as had almost happened with the 1936 ICC project), the realist narrative would have been comfortably vindicated. But we do not have that easy escape route. We have no solution but to try to reconcile the fact that States have joined an apparently incredibly 'idealist' institution with explanations derived from the national interest.

There are innumerable reasons why States would not want to join the ICC, some of them stated, others unstated by States themselves. These reasons not only range from general fears about sovereignty to awareness that the State is in the process of or will be committing crimes within the Court's jurisdiction, but also include simple scepticism, parochialism, indifference, higher priorities, and a variety of wait-and-see approaches. It is difficult to assess the rationality of not joining the ICC because so many factors may enter into account that are wholly unrelated to the Court itself. At any rate, the point seems to be that, for a good half of the international community measured by population and a good third measured by the number of States, the disadvantages of joining the ICC outweigh the advantages.

This allows us to make at least one cautionary point which is that a great many States have not considered and will not consider joining the ICC as being in their national interest. Surely that must at least partly validate the realist narrative. We know however that things may be more complex because it may be that different States will have different ways of evaluating their national interest and that the same theory may in fact yield different outcomes. The national interest is, in the end, bound to be a rather broad, fluctuating category and more of an empty container than a mechanical prism with which to anticipate State behaviour. It seems difficult to argue that States joining the ICC simply do not know better and are either not operating on the basis of national interest or are getting their national interest wrong as it were.

So what of the States that do join? Why do these at least seem to make a fundamentally different decision? Is the national interest simply not what it once was? Are they simply different States?

Note here that I am not interested in two types of international relations (IR) theories, not so much because I think that they are wrong or unhelpful *per se* but because they pursue a different goal.

The first is what is generally known as foreign policy analysis and essentially the issue of how the particular decision to join the ICC may have been taken in any given country. I acknowledge that this is an interesting angle with which to approach the issue, and I have explored it elsewhere.[7] I accept, for example, the obvious fact that, in practice, a decision to join the ICC will have often been made by all kinds of domestic political forces, such as competing ministries and, of course, civil society. But I am not interested in working out the details of that particular chemistry because, although it may tell us who in fact took the decision and even how, that is a pursuit distinct from the one in which I am interested. What I propose to do is not to engage in a sociological exercise but to evaluate how one might justify these decisions as rational within the canons of a particular tradition that takes the national interest as the determinant variable in explaining State behaviour. This rationality need not have actually been expressed by anyone in the ICC debate, although it cannot do any harm to the case I try to make if it has been. Presumably, though, this exercise is not artificial because most actors involved in foreign policy decision-making must at least partake in some commitment to a form of assessment of the national interest, although it might not be the same one or one that would lead to the same results.

The second type of theory I do not particularly use here is liberal international relations theory. Domestic liberalism has been associated with all kinds of normative outcomes on the world stage including, most notoriously, a tendency for democracies to go less frequently to war with fellow democracies. In some of its variants, liberal internationalist theory predicts that liberal States will be more likely to join international institutions. The theory does not work wonders in the case of the ICC because it fails to

---

[7] F. Mégret, 'The International Criminal Court and State Sovereignty: The 'Problem of an International Criminal Law' Re-examined', in J. Carey, J. Pritchard and W. Dunlap (eds.), *International Humanitarian Law* (New York, Transnational 2003).

explain why some major democracies – the US to quote one example but also Israel and India – would not want to join the Court. Nor does it explain why some States that do not seem particularly committed to the rule of law are nonetheless ratifying the Rome Statute. I am nevertheless quite willing to accept as a truism that, all other things being equal, stable and thriving democracies committed to the rule of law may be marginally keener to join institutions such as the Court. Certainly, the camp of those who refuse to join the Court includes a majority of authoritarian and even repressive regimes. But, regardless of whether the theory works or not, that is beside the point I am trying to make. Liberal international relations theory is still too blunt a tool because, even if it allowed us to predict that certain types of States were more likely to join the ICC, it still does not provide us (or at least not without some substantial additional work) with a comprehensive theory of why these States specifically think it in their interest to do so. Indeed, the processes whereby a commitment to liberalism domestically becomes translated into a commitment to liberal institutions internationally are among the least understood of IR theory.

Faced with the challenge of explaining ICC membership in terms of national interest, I briefly pay attention and criticize several ways in which one can choose to ignore the problem in sub-section 1. Only a conscious attempt at reconciling national interest with ICC membership, I argue in sub-section 2, can lead to satisfactory results.

1.1   The temptation to ignore the problem

1.1.1   *The temptation to minimize the problem*

One temptation is to minimize the problem of reconciling international criminal justice with sovereignty by denying that the ICC involves much of an attack on sovereignty. That argument comes in different shades but essentially seeks to soften the angles and emphasize the extent to which sovereignty is not quite what it was, that it is an outdated concept. For example, States are said to have fully internalized the fact that sovereignty is not absolute, that some crimes are simply so abhorrent that they should be judged by international tribunals speaking in the name of humanity. In other words, even before the ICC came about, we are told, the international realm had already entered an era of post-sovereignty that made it possible.

There are two problems with this approach. The first problem is the risk that one will confuse sovereignty as a concept and national interest as a variable. It may well be that sovereignty as a concept has been substantially redefined by an institution like the Court, but that still does not tell us why some States see it in their national interest to curtail their sovereignty while others do not. Second, surely the broad brush of declining sovereignty passes over too many fluctuations and local variations: obviously, many States do not feel that sovereignty is that *passé* a concept and, among these, many would be key States for the purposes of the ICC. In fact, although the ground for a successful ICC may have been prepared by a gradual softening of the contours of sovereignty as a concept, there is little doubt that the ICC takes that process a step further. The relative decline of sovereignty may have been a *cause* of the Rome Statute being adopted, but most importantly it will be a *consequence* of it being implemented so that the Court is not simply a repeat of the old world but also an attempt to create a new one in its image.

Indeed, another temptation that should be resisted is the idea that the ICC does not really affect State sovereignty that much. I argue that, on the contrary, the Rome Statute affects even the most toned down contemporary versions of sovereignty.[8] This is true of any international institution that seeks to control and modify the internal behaviour of States. As Andrew Moravcsik put it in the context of international human rights bodies, '[u]nlike international institutions governing trade, monetary, environmental, or se-curity policy, [these] institutions are not designed primarily to regulate policy externalities arising from societal interactions across borders, *but to hold*

---

[8] Of course, there is a minor linguistic conundrum here, which is that this depends on how one defines sovereignty. If one already incorporates a post-classical definition of sover-eignty as the substantially internationally controlled, limited exercise of State power, then the ICC would seem an institution in osmosis with sovereignty. But that seems like making things a bit easy for oneself. One would have to recognize that this definition is contentious and counter-intuitive and that it is precisely an issue whether sovereignty, as a result of States joining the ICC and other things, has transcended itself in such a way. Sovereignty is still by and large considered by a great many States as the exclusive, total and almost jealous exercise of power over territory. The best proof that sovereignty is still predominantly that is that so many States intend to use it to resist entering the Court regime. At most, the argument about sovereignty not being what it once was is merely an argument to the effect that sover-eignty is not what it once was *for those States that join the ICC.*

governments accountable for purely internal activities.' (emphasis added).[9]
That is unmistakably the case for the ICC, at least to the extent that many of
the crimes entering the Court's jurisdiction are crimes that can (and often
will) be committed purely internally.

But the ICC goes further than conventional international human rights
bodies in redefining sovereignty. More specifically, I would argue that, in
joining the ICC, States can be seen as making three major concessions to
the 'international community'[10] in terms of the definition of sovereignty.

Firstly, States considerably augment the likelihood that their nationals
may be tried for international law crimes at all. This is regardless of any
immunities or defences under national law or any decision to grant amnesty. This is probably the single most considerable concession by States
because the decision to try individuals for crimes under international law
would traditionally have been considered a decision that should remain primarily a largely sovereign one. Obviously such decisions, in transitional
justice contexts fraught with difficulties, have considerable political implications. The capacity to effectuate a transition that relinquishes criminal
justice, for example, has often been seen, rightly or wrongly, as the price to
pay for a peaceful return to democracy, as it was in South America in the
1980s. Regardless of the merits of that position, the ICC takes away any
form of State discretion in such matters.

Secondly, States accept the possibility that trials of their nationals may
in some circumstances occur before an *international* criminal tribunal rather
than before their own jurisdictions. Whatever the safeguards of complementarity, States joining the ICC must know that this is at least a theoretical possibility. This is in itself a further problematic dimension for the

---

[9] Moravcsik (n. 1) 217.

[10] Here the term 'international community' will be used in quotation marks to recognize the fact that this term is itself loaded with ideological presuppositions and is hardly
uncontentious as an empirical reality. Note, however, that I am not interested for the purposes of this article in whether such a thing as the 'international community' exists or not.
Rather, I will be content with suggesting that, if it existed, it would provide an interesting
way of looking at the problem of complementarity. Indeed, it is sufficient for my exploration that the 'international community' as an idea, rather than as an empirical reality, is
reasonably successful in expressing our intuition of something like it that might exist. I also
consider that the 'international community' does not exist in a void and is also partly
perfomatively realized through its various actual and theoretical instantiations.

sovereign: it means that there is a very real risk that some of the State's nationals will be tried internationally, with the ensuing international publicity and attention, not to mention the added opprobrium of being tried by a tribunal that claims to represent a large segment of the international community. Not only will States not decide whether certain individuals should be tried, but, if they lose control of a case to the ICC, they will also have very little influence on how these crimes get tried. This includes problems of disclosure of information regarding sensitive national security issues. International trials also mean that these individuals will be prosecuted according to international standards for a fair trial which, although they may represent the current State of what international law requires, will not be particularly culturally sensitive and, for example, may not mimic whatever legal tradition in which the national law is embedded.

Thirdly, States accept the possibility that, in pursuance of the previous possibility, the ICC may be called upon to examine the functioning of their national jurisdictions and, in the process, find these wanting, notably through the application of the Rome Statute's admissibility requirements. This – and I will return in more detail to the nature of complementarity in due course – is perhaps in itself one of the worst assaults on sovereignty there is, adding insult to injury by implicitly accusing a domestic system of not being up to its international obligations to stand up to impunity. Essentially, in that context, the accusation shifts from the individual accused of having committed an international crime to the State accused of having tolerated it by not trying him effectively.

Therefore, as can be seen, there is nothing negligible about the sacrifice of sovereignty involved in joining the ICC. This is all the more so because joining the ICC is a substantially more irreversible move than, for example, recognizing the International Court of Justice's compulsory jurisdiction.[11] What is at stake seems to be more than a simple entanglement of sovereignty in one more web of obligations, one more international regime. At

---

[11] In theory, States can leave the ICC by giving a one year notice pursuant to Art. 127 of the Rome Statute of the International Criminal Court (Rome Statute) (adopted 17 July 1998, entered into force 1 July 2002) UN Doc. A/CONF.183/9. In practice, because of the nature of the issues involved, it seems highly unlikely (although of course not impossible) that States would do such a thing. This raises the stakes even more because joining the ICC will appear as a fairly permanent commitment.

the very least, the ICC makes an implicit claim to changing the nature of State sovereignty. I posit that, as a result, in terms of national interest, it is and will be the unmistakable goal of any State joining the ICC to avoid these perceived embarrassments to its sovereignty at all costs. So arguments about why States join the ICC have no choice but to argue why States join the ICC *despite the clear modification of sovereignty that becoming a Party to the ICC entails and the consequent risk to a State's national interest*.

1.1.2   *The temptation to avoid the problem*

One possible way to resolve the paradox is simply to resort to irrationalist explanations and to say that States do not know better or are not joining the ICC seriously. Domestic agendas may be a factor here. For example, the decision by President William J. Clinton to sign the Rome Statute in the dying days of his administration was obviously meant more as a thorn in the heels of the next administration than as a true commitment to the ICC. External factors and pressures also play a role. It is conceivable that some small States under pressure from international civil society and with limited diplomatic resources will join the ICC without a rigorous assessment of all the risks involved. We should perhaps not assume too readily that we are always dealing with highly trained diplomatic services committed to computing every risk and benefit into the equation with a conservative eye on the national interest.

While such explanations may account for a very small portion of the decisions to join, they nonetheless seem at most of marginal relevance and difficult to demonstrate. It is difficult to believe that all but a few States would join the ICC after anything short of a reasonably thorough assessment of the risks to the national interest involved. At any rate, in a good social-scientific manner and without discounting totally the role of the stochastic, it seems preferable in the great majority of cases to assume that States join the ICC for *rational* reasons.

1.2   The need for an explanation in terms of national interest

1.2.1   *The idealist stance*

Within rationalist types of explanations, the first extreme is unashamedly idealist or normativist. Essentially, it amounts to saying something to the effect that, after centuries of war, violence and grief, States have finally woken up to the realization that untrammelled sovereignty, when it comes to human rights and humanitarian law, is simply either a source of unmitigated evil or not in their best interest. According to that story, States have become deeply suspicious of themselves and more and more willing to surrender to some higher and more trustworthy entity prerogatives that they have come to see as an embarrassing remnant of their violent pasts. In fact, States have internalized that logic to such a degree that they almost cease to think like States and already behave as constituent entities of a global (albeit minimal) cosmopolis in the making. The national interest, essentially, is written off as an explanatory variable or is satisfied by the suggestion that, in surrendering a large part of its sovereignty, a State participates in the advent of a global federation of States.

Let me state clearly from the outset that I think these explanations are deeply unsatisfying, except to explain perhaps why the Vatican is joining the ICC. Such reasoning may be prevalent within international civil society, some governments may be more sensitive to it than others and individuals within diplomatic delegations may have some commitment to the values thereby embodied. But it seems very unlikely that any foreign service would think exclusively in these terms. It is obvious that some States will join treaties on the basis of what Oona Hathaway has described as the 'normative view'[12] to treaty adherence, one in which 'the cost of commitment is less important than norms'.[13] For all kinds of domestic reasons, some States may be more prone to embrace normative causes internationally than others. But, even if in the absolute some States' interests 'are determined predominantly by their normative commitments',[14] norms are always going to be simply one element in a larger equation. Surely the idea

---

[12] Hathaway (n. 2) 1829.
[13] Ibid.
[14] Ibid. 1830.

that the cost of commitment is less important than norms is not an absolute policy constraint so that even respect for a minor norm would oblige the State to incur significant costs in terms of its national interest. It is, instead, an equation that has to be reassessed in each and every case where, notwithstanding a substantive normative commitment *ceteris paribus*, that commitment may be trumped by more significant fears about costs. *There is a difference between the idea of certain values shaping the national interest and these values becoming a substitute for it.* Such a stance simply asks us to concede too much with little evidence to buttress its case.

The explanation would be more convincing if, in other fields, State behaviour towards the end of the 20th century and the beginning of the 21st edged more systematically towards this kind of mature sovereignty. The truth, in fact, seems much more complex, and, among States joining the ICC, very few would not be vulnerable to accusations that they were violating or neglecting human rights or operating externally in a way that seemed deeply incompatible with an unmitigated commitment to international law.

The more sophisticated version of the idealist stance is broadly social-contractarian in nature. The idea here is that States suffer from the fact that international crimes are not repressed. A negative externality is created by the fact that States cannot rely on other States to repress international crimes consistently. In some cases, States will be reluctant to take the first step, for example, by trying their own nationals, as long as other States do not do the same because they feel they may be putting themselves at a comparative disadvantage. Essentially, the ICC solves a classic problem of cooperation. The ICC ensures the delivery of a global public good – no impunity for international crimes – in exchange for which States are willing to relinquish some of their sovereignty. Occasionally, as in any criminal justice system, nationals of States Parties may be exposed to the Court's jurisdiction but, overall, the assumption is that they benefit from the security conferred upon the system as a result. Their interest is thus maximized.

Obviously this explanation of the ICC is appealing, but it has several problematic features. First, it does not really resolve the problem of transition from one system to another. Obviously all States might have an interest in an already existing system of international criminal justice, but not all States would have an interest in being the first to join such a system. So the theory fails to account for the 'big bang' of international criminal justice. Second, it neglects the extent to which all States do not stand to gain equally from joining the ICC. Clearly a State with a 'criminal' potential (and surely this must be at least partly foreseeable by the State itself) has considerably more to lose than a State that sees itself as by and large law-abiding. Third, the reasoning does not explain how the system would avoid free-riding (presumably, non-States Parties will benefit from the Court's existence in terms of added respect for the international rule of law without actually having to pay the price). Fourth, the reasoning is, in my view, more a description of how the ICC might be seen once it has been created than an explanation of how the ICC is created.

The 'idealist' explanation of why States would want to join the ICC, therefore, seems to suffer from all the defects that have long been highlighted as being those of idealism in IR. Quite often, in fact, the idealist discourse that surrounds the ICC will obfuscate a proper exploration of why States might realistically want to join the ICC by too closely equating the 'ought' and the 'is' and will even do a disservice to the cause of international criminal justice.

It seems necessary, therefore, to move beyond these idealist explanations and to start from more squarely grounded assumptions about the national interest. On what unmistakably 'realist' grounds might a State want to join the ICC?

1.2.2 *Reconciling the ICC with the national interest*

Obviously, how one assesses what rational reasons a State might have to join the ICC is not epistemologically unproblematic, and the national interest as a concept is itself fraught with difficulty. By national interest, I do not mean simply the old realist concept of the national interest expressed in terms of power, and part of my making a big concession to the fundamental intuitions of realism is that I am ready to be flexible about the definitions of some of its core concepts. There are no tanks to be had in joining the ICC, no strategic advantage, no natural resources, no access to the sea. But I do understand the national interest as meaning a certain sense of doing things not simply *out of principle but out of a desire to maximize benefits even if doing so incurs costs* (whatever these may be).

There are all kinds of reasons why a State might want to join the ICC which, while rational, have nothing to do with the ICC *per se* or with a serious assessment of the opportunities and dangers it really entails. For example, it is notorious that ratifying the Rome Statute has become part of a package of international respectability that the European Union (EU) is promoting energetically. To the extent that the EU is a large commercial partner or aid donor, it may be that ratifying the Statute is simply an offer some States cannot refuse because so much seems to hang in the balance if they do. States are generally prone to discount the value of the future in order to reap short-term benefits: When the threats seem distant and the immediate benefits tangible, it is not hard to see which way most governments would go. It is probable that this is a factor that helps to explain why at least some States have joined the ICC.

It is worth noting, however, that even the EU has fallen short of making aid allocation conditional upon ratification of the Statute. Indeed, overall, I would still contend that perhaps, even for the States mentioned above and certainly for most others, the most relevant factors in deciding to join have to do with how joining the ICC per se will affect the national interest.

Specifically, I contend that an assessment of whether it is in a State's interest to join the ICC will above all hinge upon how that State evaluates how the Court's jurisdictional set-up will play out in its case. In this respect obviously all States are not equal before the ICC in terms of how much they have to win and lose in that respect.[15] The most general formula of how the national interest is likely to be computed in such cases encompasses both an evaluation of the propensity to commit crimes under international law and a vulnerability to being the victim of such crimes. Specifically, two factors are relevant here: First, the likelihood that a State's nationals – particularly those in an official position and especially when implementing a State policy – will commit international crimes; second, the likelihood that international crimes will be committed on a State's territory or against its nationals.[16]

---

[15] This seems to run contrary to Andrew Moravcsik's assumption that 'the inconvenience governments face is constant (or randomly distributed)'. Moravcsik (n. 1) 228. See Hathaway's treatment of the 'sovereignty view' of the costs of commitment. Hathaway (n. 2) 1827-28. In contrast to Hathaway, though, I tend to understand Moravcsik's assumption as a methodological hypothesis rather than one that claims to be empirically substantiated.

[16] Although in the latter case that is an insufficient basis for the ICC to satisfy the preconditions for jurisdiction.

These two speculations point to two different concerns: One is for a State to protect itself from the risk of its nationals being prosecuted; the second is to protect its population and territory from the commission of international crimes by raising the likelihood that such crimes are prosecuted. One is a reason to hesitate joining the ICC; the other is a reason to become a party to it.

There are all kinds of ways in which these two factors can be combined, depending on the historical, political and sociological mix of any given State and its international position. At the point of ratification, in fact, the State must juggle a very complex series of potentially conflicting imperatives, a set of imperatives that is substantially more complex than those entailed by joining an international human rights treaty for example.[17] Indeed, there are clearly two axes upon which the decision to join must be made: one international, the other domestic.

On the international axis, the decision to join the ICC is a function of the likelihood that a State's nationals will commit crimes abroad and the likelihood that foreign nationals will commit international crimes on the territory of the State Party. At one extreme, a State with a high risk of committing international crimes on the territory of other States but a low risk of having international crimes committed by others on its territory will, in all likelihood, not want to join the ICC at all. It will, in other words, see only disadvantages and no benefits of joining. At the other extreme, a State which thinks of itself or its nationals as very unlikely to commit international crimes but quite likely to have such crimes committed on its territory by nationals of other States will be a very plausible candidate for joining the Court. In fact, a State whose nationals are very unlikely to commit international crimes will probably want to join the ICC regardless of whether there is any risk of

---

[17] In that respect the framework of international criminal law is distinct from that of international human rights law (but closer to that of international humanitarian law). In the context of international human rights law, there is no (or very little) fear that failure to respect international human rights obligations by one State will spill over or have any other effect in another State. This means that the benefits and costs of joining an international human rights regime are assessed very much in terms of purely domestic consequences. In the context of international criminal law, at least some of the international crimes (aggression, war crimes committed in international armed conflict, crimes against humanity and even genocide) will be committed across borders so that, in joining the ICC, States must also calculate how ratification will affect their relative position *vis-à-vis* other States.

such crimes being committed on its territory. If joining the ICC is costless, then a State might as well join, if only for the sake of constraining the margin of freedom of other States in their international dealings with third States.

It would be wrong, however, to think too much in interstate terms when it comes to the ICC. Although some crimes within the Court's jurisdiction are inherently international (aggression, war crimes in international armed conflict) and most can be committed in an international context (for example, an interstate war resulting in the commission of genocide or crimes against humanity), those crimes are not necessarily at the forefront of the Court's jurisdiction (aggression, for one, is still awaiting a definition) and have tended to recede in the case law of the *ad hoc* tribunals of the 1990s (as opposed to Nuremberg and Tokyo). Most importantly, in fact, in addition to those few crimes that are inherently internal (war crimes committed in non-international armed conflict), most crimes entering the Court's jurisdiction will be likely to have been committed in almost exclusively internal settings (genocide and crimes against humanity tend to be largely internal phenomena). So in addition to evaluating its national interest in international terms, States have to assess the significance of joining the ICC domestically (this type of reasoning is familiar to those who have studied States' motivations for ratifying human rights or humanitarian law treaties, except that here the existence of a proper enforcement mechanism makes that decision even more sensitive because it is more than a formal decision).

For a State which thinks that it is very unlikely that international crimes will be committed in a purely 'domestic' fashion on its territory, the 'internal' factor is neutral. The situation of a State which thinks that international crimes will be committed internally is more complex, depending on whether that State thinks that these crimes will be committed by itself (that is by the current government), by some rebellious force on its territory or by a future government. One can confidently predict that the more a government thinks that crimes will be committed 'by others' and that joining the ICC is a means of protecting itself against such others, the more likely a State is to want to join the ICC.

So the State must simultaneously assess these two equations: How will the ICC's jurisdiction play out internationally and domestically? It may be that the advantages gained internationally by joining the ICC will more than offset the potential domestic costs or vice versa. In both situations reviewed above, note that I have suggested extreme scenarios where the issue is whether a State will commit international crimes or have international crimes committed against itself at all. In practice, the evaluation will be one that works in terms of probabilities and the likelihood in the short-, mid- and long-term, making evaluations of whether it is in a State's interest to join the Court particularly delicate.

Note, however, that, in case of doubt (a situation likely to arise often), States are likely not to join. This is partly because States are risk averse creatures, more likely to minimize their costs than to take chances to maximize their benefits. It is also because these two considerations – protecting its nationals and territory from international crimes and avoiding prosecution of its nationals – are not exactly on par, especially if seen through a realist lens keen on avoiding the worst case scenario. Increasing the prospect that crimes committed on a State's territory by others are prosecuted is not necessarily a negligible policy goal. In so doing, the State may arguably contribute to 'sanctuarizing' its territory from the commission of international crimes by earmarking it internationally as one in which perpetrators of international crimes do so at their peril because the prospect of prosecution is backed by the credible threat of the ICC, acting as a sort of supranational deterrent. I would argue, however, that it will be more crucial in terms of national interest for a State to avoid some of its nationals being prosecuted for international crimes than simply to know that international crimes committed on its territory by others will be prosecuted. The advantage gained in the former case is relatively theoretical because it is unlikely that deterrence would work very effectively in that specific a way;[18] the inconvenience incurred in the latter is clear and direct, as I have already emphasized.[19]

---

[18] Whether international criminal justice has a deterrent effect is of course a big debate in itself. After high hopes were invested in the idea in the early days of the development of international criminal tribunals, the emerging consensus seems to be that, if deterrence works at all in the context of the tribunals, it is only in the most general of ways and in the very long-term. Few, in other words, would argue that a more credible threat of prosecution for international crimes will actually be an effective way of protecting a State's territory or nationals from the commission of such crimes.

[19] After all, it is not as if a State can expect a considerable amount from the fact that international crimes committed on its territory will be prosecuted. If anything, what will be

At any rate, if this assessment is correct, one overriding truth seems to emerge, which henceforth will be at the heart of this essay: The States most likely to join the ICC are by far, all other things being equal, essentially those who do not commit or are not likely to commit international crimes. Whether it is open to any State to think in such terms and whether history has not, in a sense, taught us that no State is ever entirely immune from the danger of spiralling into violence is open to question. But it should be said that, to the extent that it is difficult to imagine San Marino, for example, embarking tomorrow on a campaign of genocide, the explanation must hold true for at least some States.

Indeed, regardless of the position one takes on the issue of predictability of criminal behaviour, it suffices to explain why States might want to join (as opposed to why States might be right to join) that, to their best calculations, they think of themselves and of their joining the ICC in such a way. At any rate, many States must know that, barring any absolutely unforeseen circumstances, it is a very legitimate extrapolation that, for example, being stable societies that are not particularly involved in hegemonic or bellicose pursuits, they will not engage in any of the activities that enter the Court's jurisdiction. In such a situation, there is no risk involved in joining the ICC so States might as well reap the benefits. Such States have *no reason not to join the ICC* and probably some marginal reason for doing so. If there are hardly any costs, then even marginal benefits, such as the relatively minor reputational benefit of looking virtuous internationally, start to look comparatively worth having. A cynic might remark that it is particularly those States that are most likely to succumb to the illusion that they are adhering with a view to enhancing international norms and justice, when all they are in fact doing is something that they would have done anyhow and which maximizes their national interest.

Note, in addition, that even States that think their nationals in official positions may occasionally commit international crimes might still want to join the ICC. There is a difference between the possibility that a State's nationals might commit international crimes and the possibility that they be

---

obtained is less a deterrent effect (as is often a little precipitously assumed) than the moral comfort of having the international community's law on its side. So we would have to assess the prospect of a State's own nationals being prosecuted as the *key variable* in explaining why States join the ICC or not in terms of its national interest.

prosecuted internationally by the ICC. It is now well understood that the ICC will only judge the worst crimes which, by all accounts, will only be a fraction (and possibly a very small fraction) of all crimes over which the Court might conceivably exercise jurisdiction. So it is very possible that, while a State might conceive of its nationals being involved in international crimes, it would calculate that these crimes would never at any given point in time be the worst ones worthy of being prosecuted internationally.

This sort of intermediary hypothesis might well account, for example, for the position of the bigger, but relatively virtuous, military powers. France and the United Kingdom (UK), contrary to what seems to be the reasoning of the US, may suspect that the breadth of their military involvement in many of the world's hotspots will sooner or later expose them to accusations that their nationals have committed international crimes, but they may also calculate that, as States that see themselves as unlikely ever to be engaged in a systematic, State-sponsored campaign of international criminality, such crimes are likely to escape the necessarily selective scrutiny of the ICC's Prosecutor.

As a result, there is a very real possibility that the ICC would be an institution composed exclusively of virtuous States. It is an open question, however, whether any State in joining the ICC can ever be entirely sure that its nationals will not commit crimes that catch the Prosecutor's attention. Indeed, note the following interesting phenomenon: The view that the ICC is relatively safe for virtuous countries is premised on the idea that there will always be worse offenders from States Parties to the Statute to keep the Prosecutor busy. But, if only virtuous States joined the ICC, then the level of crimes that would catch the Prosecutor's attention would lower considerably so that it may become difficult to avoid prosecutions even for minor international crimes (institutions hate to sit idly by so we can count on the Prosecutor to lower the threshold).

The point seems to be that the definition of the worst crimes is not an absolute but a relative notion: There will always be individuals who at any one time or place will have committed the worst crimes over which the ICC could exercise jurisdiction, even though these may not (and probably will not) be the worst crimes that are committed in the world at that time. So apart from a quite small minority of 'absolutely virtuous' States, most States must know that joining the ICC involves a risk that some crimes committed by their nationals may be prosecuted.

In fact, quite contrary to realist expectations, even a cursory study of States Parties to the ICC shows that a number of them have, in fact, a significant incidence and prospect of international crimes being committed on their territory and/or by their nationals in the coming years (Congo and Colombia come to mind).[20] Quite rapidly in fact, unless one is willing simply to buy the heroic, idealist narrative of how the ICC came about, one seems to run into intractable difficulties that a more traditional realist account does not seem to allow us to overcome. Can a middle way between these two options nonetheless be found?

2.   AN EXPLORATION OF THE NATURE OF COMPLEMENTARITY

While adhering to our core assumption about the need to explain how joining the ICC might be construed in terms of national interest, it is necessary at this point to start parting company with the more narrow aspects of realism. The obvious deficiency of realism when explaining why even States facing significant risks of having their nationals commit international crimes might join the ICC is that it fails to detect certain elements in the Rome Statute that might nonetheless allow States to bridge the gap between a commitment to international criminal justice and the national interest. In discounting the importance of the law, realist discourse about the ICC tends to obscure the fact that the problem is not explaining why States would not want to join *any* permanent and potentially universal international criminal court but why they would want to join *this* particular court.

---

[20] Hathaway's suggestion that 'one would expect that treaties with stronger enforcement and monitoring provisions would exhibit a pattern of ratification close to what rationalists and normativists would predict' seems reasonably borne out by the ICC experience. Hathaway (n. 2) 1835. Clearly the ICC is just such a treaty with stronger enforcement and monitoring provisions and has obtained the support of a significant number of virtuous States (the normative approach) and very few States for whom the cost of commitment would seem important (the rationalist approach). Even in the case of the ICC, though, there are some States joining the Court who seem *a priori* as if their commitment to international norms is not great and as if they could incur significant costs. It is this intermediary category of States that is the most interesting and which seems to be explained fully by neither the normative nor rationalist approaches.

Instead, what I want to do is emphasize how the national interest is necessarily constructed and how its formulation is influenced by normative considerations, which are themselves shaped by the various discrete forms the law takes. In contrast to a position of the law as neutral on the formulation of the national interest, I want to show the importance of certain 'legal devices' in nudging the formulation of State interest in certain directions. I want, in other words, to highlight a specifically 'legal' take on the explanation of why States might want to join the ICC. Specifically, I want to focus on how complementarity as a legal regime is uniquely suited to enticing States to join the ICC even when a State might think of its nationals as otherwise at risk of prosecution.

Complementarity's attitude toward and implicit construction of sovereignty is very ambivalent. On the one hand, complementarity does represent a minimal recognition of the legitimacy of State sovereignty. Complementarity is a presumption in favour of national jurisdiction. In being a presumption, it is also more than that: It is an implicit, normative and substantive preference for the work of national jurisdictions in dealing with international crimes. The work of the Rome Conference and the earlier debates are testimony to the profound bias of States in favour of national, contextual solutions to what is by and large still perceived as an issue that is predominantly national (for example a transitional issue).

On the other hand, complementarity is also a potent threat to State sovereignty. The price of the international community's recognition of the priority of national jurisdictions is that the ICC may exercise its jurisdiction only if that priority is not put to good use. If the relationship between national jurisdictions and the ICC had been one of primacy of national jurisdictions (that is the exact inverted image of the set-up of the *ad hoc* international criminal tribunals), then States would have had a lot less to fear. As it is, however, complementarity leaves a threatening sword of Damocles hanging over national judiciaries.

Again, if we think in realist terms of the worst possible scenario, the danger of an ICC prosecution will be seen as the deciding factor rather than the relatively nominal recognition of the priority of States to prosecute international crimes. Why would States want to put themselves in a position where, notwithstanding the international community's recognition of their right to a 'first strike' against international crimes, they expose themselves to losing jurisdiction over often politically sensitive cases?

I want to examine how this dual nature of complementarity – complementarity as recognition of sovereignty versus complementarity as a threat to sovereignty – is not only the defining characteristic of the ICC, as all international lawyers readily acknowledge, but also the key element in any explanation of why States would want to join the Court. I propose to do this by distinguishing between two different types of States which I refer to as 'quasi-virtuous' and 'hesitantly virtuous' States.[21]

The first type is less problematic and can be treated by way of introduction. 'Quasi-virtuous' States, or 'almost virtuous' States, I define as *States which can conceive that their nationals might commit international crimes but who cannot conceive that they would not want to try them*. Even if hardly any State can be totally immunized from the possibility of its nationals committing international crimes in the more or less distant future, some States must at least assume that such crimes would be exceptional and marginal (typically, an isolated war crime rather than a systematic campaign of genocide). As a result, these States will probably be relatively certain that their national legal systems would be up to the challenge of trying them.

The States I have in mind in this respect are, for example, EU Member States, all of which have come strongly in favour of the ICC. For these and others, there are essentially very few costs and some marginal benefits to be had in joining the Court. These States know that, even if their nationals commit international crimes that the Prosecutor would want to prosecute, they will never have to incur the disgrace of having some of their nationals prosecuted internationally because they can effectively pre-empt such an outcome by judging them domestically. These are typically States that are joining a treaty regime that 'do[es] not require them to depart from what they would have done in its absence'.[22] Needless to say, EU Member States do not deserve great merit in joining the ICC because they have so little to lose from doing so.

In addition to the absence of significant costs, there are at least some marginally symbolic benefits associated with joining the Court. These States

---

[21] Note that in using these terms I am not making a point that this is indeed what these States are, but merely that they perceive themselves as such. No moral judgment is involved.

[22] G.W. Downs, D. Rocke and P. Barsoom, 'Is the Good News About Compliance Good News About Cooperation?', 50 *Intl Organization* (1996), 379, 383.

have incorporated to a high degree (at least rhetorically) the idea that their foreign policy should abide by international human rights norms. Public opinion will be satisfied that the 'right' decision has been made, and elites will be vindicated in their conception of Europe's process of constructing its identity as an emerging world power committed to the global spread of human rights and the international rule of law. Joining the Court *en masse* also means that the ICC can become a very European institution, one which European States have a good chance of guiding in a direction that conforms to their fundamental vision of the international order.

In fact, not joining the ICC is almost not an option for EU Member States because it would put them starkly at odds with some their stated international goals. Not joining the ICC would amount to conceding the possibility that one might be 'unwilling or unable'[23] to try international crimes, an almost inconceivable possibility in contemporary Europe. Indeed, the existence of complementarity opens up this most powerful of rhetorical tricks, one which civil society has been prompt to put to good use: 'If such and such State is so committed to the fight against impunity and therefore has nothing to lose by joining the ICC, then why is it not joining the Court?' It is this type of reasoning that eventually made France's reservations *vis-à-vis* the ICC at the Rome Conference untenable and led that country to ratify the Statute.

So complementarity does account for the fact that a number of quasi-virtuous States will join the ICC. These States join confident in the belief that they will always be on the good side of ICC prosecutions. But this in turn raises some eminently troubling questions for the Court. If the only States that join the ICC are virtuous and almost virtuous States, then what is left of the ICC's role? An ICC composed exclusively of States whose nationals do not commit international crimes or whose national jurisdictions face no risk of not dealing with the international crimes committed would be a toothless Court, a semblance of Court. It would never try any cases either for lack of a crime or for lack of a failure of national jurisdictions. The Court would be a club of virtuous States, a Scandinavian or an EU Court, confident in its virtue at the expense of any meaningful role on the international scene.

---

[23] Rome Statute (n. 11) Art. 17 para. 1a.

Note that this is different from saying, as is often done, that an ideal ICC is an ICC that will not have to try any cases because it will force States pre-emptively to do so. That is true but not if the ICC's inactivity results from the fact that its only members are engaging in domestic prosecutions of international crimes virtuously and without any prompting. If that were the case, then the Court would simply be useless and expensive international machinery. The ICC's relative lack of judicial activity will only be an indicator of success if it follows from the Court's ability to force States that would not otherwise have the impetus to conduct diligent prosecutions to do so. Thus, if the ICC is to be a significant institution at all, it must somehow be able to entice States that are somewhat less than quasi-virtuous to ratify the Rome Statute.

It may be, and I have in fact argued this elsewhere,[24] that the ICC will fail in doing so and indeed be precisely such a useless and expensive international machine. But this is not specifically what I am interested in here. I am interested in the question: *What kind of concept of the national interest might one have to come up with to make the case that States other than virtuous or almost virtuous ones might join the Court?* It may be that such a theory will be so farfetched that one can confidently predict that the Court will never attract such States' membership, but I remain interested in formulating the conditions under which joining might appear at least minimally rational and plausible.

If there is a category of States that fits the description of what I have in mind then these are what I will describe as hesitantly virtuous States. I define 'hesitantly virtuous' States as that – probably relatively rare – breed of States which, on the one hand, are not able to guarantee that their legal systems would effectively prosecute international crimes committed by their nationals (meaning that they can provide the ICC with a case load), but, on the other hand, are nonetheless committed to the long-term goal of fighting impunity (otherwise they would simply not join at all). Is there any theory that could explain why such crucial States would want to join the ICC?

My argument is that joining a complementarity-based ICC can only be understood as a process of 'international constitutionalization' whereby hesitantly virtuous States willingly put themselves in a position *where they*

---

[24] Mégret (n. 6).

will have no choice but to prosecute international crimes nationally. In order to make that point, I draw heavily on work on the nature of rationality, including political rationality, particularly as pioneered by Jon Elster in his groundbreaking book *Ulysses and the Sirens: Studies in Rationality and Irrationality*.[25]

Specifically, I propose a three-stage model: complementarity as constitutionalization, complementarity as internationalization and complementarity as institutionalization. First, I introduce the ideas of intertemporal commitments and of the ICC as being essentially a means for States to constitutionalize a commitment to fight impunity; second, I show how, following the example of international human rights courts, the ICC represents an attempt to guarantee that commitment internationally; third, I argue that the specificity of the ICC, compared to such international human rights courts, lies in a highly unusual process of transfer and potential substitution of sovereign functions through complementarity. Joining the ICC for hesitantly virtuous States can only be understood as a combination of all three of these processes, and only the combination of all three is peculiar to the Court.

Finally, I will top this three-tier analysis with a more detailed doctrinal construction of the concept of complementarity, one that hopefully makes sense of all the preceding developments in a more dynamic way to show how complementarity might allow the Court eventually to solidify into something very different from what States had initially contemplated.

2.1   Constitutionalization: complementarity as intertemporal commitment

Let us begin by stating our hypothesis in the following way. As suggested, hesitantly virtuous States are those who, for all their uncertainty about the future and the ultimate strength of their own resolve, are, in principle, committed in the present to ensure themselves against reversals in their own will. This is not altogether implausible. It is beyond doubt that some States have undergone extremely traumatic experiences, as a result of interna-

---

[25] J. Elster, *Ulysses and the Sirens: Studies in Rationality and Irrationality* (Cambridge, Cambridge University Press 1979).

tional crimes being committed on their territory or by or against their nationals, which have profoundly shaped their identity (Rwanda comes to mind for example). It is also fair to say that, for at least some of these States, avoiding a repeat of such experiences is considered, perhaps even far and above the strict maintenance of traditional sovereignty, a fundamental goal of national policy.[26]

Let us start with an easy, one-dimensional, domestic model that can begin to capture some of the logic of complementarity. A traditional way of avoiding a repeat of particularly traumatic events would have been through a process of constitutionalization. The aim of processes of constitutionalization is, essentially, to keep certain values or commitments from outside the ordinary fray of politics. Some values are perceived as sufficiently important that they are embodied in documents (or more rarely in unwritten normative regimes) that have superior value in the hierarchy of norms and which, moreover, are either theoretically impossible to change or at least much more difficult to change than ordinary laws. Ensuring that 'international crimes are not committed by one's nationals or on one's territory' might be such a value, and the 'guarantee that national jurisdictions will try international crimes' might be a means of achieving it, as well as a value in itself.

One particularly fruitful way of looking at constitutions and why they emerge is to see them as helping to solve problems of intertemporality. Essentially, the State in the present, having resolved that certain norms are particularly essential to the polity but fearing that, in different and possibly difficult circumstances, it may well be tempted to renounce these very values, seeks to bind itself to adhere to these norms in the future. Hence constitutions emerge so that a given preference expressed at time 't' will continue binding the State at time 't + t'. In the context of international crimes, the idea is that the State might 'protect itself against the temptation of commit-

---

[26] This ideal *entre-deux* as States with a soft spot for international judicial institutions was well perceived by Moravcsik who sees that a State is most likely to support international human rights bodies in a postwar period if it is 'firmly committed to democratic governance but faces strong internal challenges that may threaten it in the future.' Moravcsik (n. 1) 228. That is, '*the strongest support for binding human rights regimes should come not from established democracies but from recently established and potentially unstable democracies.*' Moravcsik (n. 1) 228-229.

ting international crimes and then of not trying them domestically in the future'.

One risk with such explanations, however, is that they will focus, as is the traditional way of international law, on the State as a unitary, homogeneous and internally inscrutable actor (ironically, in flagrant disregard of international criminal law's own State-deconstructivist and individual-methodological epistemology). It is true that, for the purposes of both domestic and international law, it is the State as the State *qua* State that undergoes processes of constitutionalization. Formally, it is undeniable that the State is binding itself and not whatever legislative assembly or government is responsible for actually doing so.

But the State in this context is only a useful fiction. In practice, it is always one particular instantiation of the State as represented by one government that seeks to bind the State in the future – namely other governments. This can allow us to make better sense of the process of joining the ICC. There are two ways one can look at the issue.

The first is as the process by which certain social groups in society (represented by a government) see themselves as potentially vulnerable to the commission of international crimes and seek to protect themselves against other social groups that may come to power in that State in the future. If one understands constitutionalization in that simple way, then there is no longer any contradiction between the fact that a State will join the ICC and the fact that it may well commit international crimes. This simply means that some groups in power at a given time clearly care more about protecting the State against the scourge of impunity than they do about the potential risk to the State of being dragged before an international judicial body.

But there is a second and more intriguing – although, again, not wholly implausible – way in which the process of constitutionalization can be interpreted. It may well be that the government that makes the decision to bind the State by joining the ICC and the one that is feared may commit international crimes tomorrow will in fact turn out to be one and the same. In fact, a government at a moment 't' may actually know that, at a moment 't + t1' in the more or less distant future, it (or its political successors) may risk both committing international crimes and being tempted not to prosecute them. Indeed, in an international crime-prone society in which the commission of crimes is linked to complex patterns of recursive violence, it will certainly be difficult for a government to be 100 per cent sure that, if international crimes are committed, they will always be committed by the other side. In fact, in all likelihood, through processes of retaliation and the like, and even though one side may end up bearing the brunt of guilt in committing international crimes, it is rare that violations will not be committed by both sides.

Moreover, even if a given government thinks of itself as essentially constraining future governments rather than itself, there is always an element of reflexiveness involved in joining the ICC. In the end, regardless of domestic rationale, the government that decides to join is effectively binding the State *lato sensu*, in all its fictitious continuity. To the extent that any government is at least implicitly the depositary of the protection of that State's long-term interest, there is at least something intriguing about the fact that a government would willingly put that State at risk of international prosecutions.

What this amounts to is the opening up of the apparently bizarre possibility that a government would, to an extent, seek to protect itself against itself by making sure once and for all that, even if it were to commit international crimes in the future, it would effectively have put itself in a situation where, thanks to complementarity, it had no choice but to prosecute them. This might of course seem counter-intuitive and even paradoxical at first. One might understand why a government would want to bind its successors from opposite sides, but why would a government want to bind itself in the future? Can a government not trust itself or its like-minded successors to make the right decisions?

As it happens, this logic is less flawed or bizarre than it might seem at first. The reason why it may appear flawed to us is that we assume that the State always wants as much freedom as possible in defining its preferences at any given time. But in fact, the State may also, for example in light of past events, be reasonably sceptical of itself and its own changing preferences and may want to guarantee itself against future fluctuations in its resolve. Probably, the key contribution to our understanding of such complex patterns of rationality was made by Jon Elster[27] (and before him by Spinoza from whom the idea was borrowed). The point of Ulysses asking his sailors to tie him to the mast and not to untie him even if he were to beg them to do so was that Ulysses wanted to make sure that he would protect

---

[27] Elster (n. 25).

himself against his own temptation to join the sirens which, in the present, he could appreciate would have led to his death.

Elster's use of the tale of Ulysses as a metaphor for precommitment enlightens us about the possibility that individuals will make decisions that will bind them in the future, *even against their own will* as expressed in the future. Although applying this reasoning to polities is by no means unproblematic, Elster has suggested this metaphor as the paradigm for constitutions. In adopting constitutions at a given time, a State seeks to limit substantially the flexibility of future governments to adopt policies that would be contrary to certain values considered central to the polity at the time the constitutional commitment was formulated.

There is nothing utopian about such a scheme, even internationally. A typical example of such logic would be the German and Japanese constitutions which forbade troops from these countries from ever participating in external military operations, even though occasionally such participation might obviously be in these States' interest. The logic here seems to be the prudential one that the best way never to commit aggression or war crimes in international armed conflict is to remove the possibility *ab initio* of ever having recourse to force outside one's territory. In such a way, both Germany and Japan seemed to have effectively exorcised a flagrantly hegemonic and militaristic past that might have returned to haunt them otherwise.

In this manner, we can begin to make sense of a hesitantly virtuous State joining the ICC without resorting to irrationalist explanations. It is conceivable that such States would join the ICC because they want to make sure that either committing international crimes or being tempted not to try them is not an option. A not inconsequential benefit of such an intertemporal commitment is that it maximizes the promise and credibility of deterrence by ensuring that those who commit international crimes (whether they be that State's nationals or acting on its territory) will know that impunity will not be a likely option.[28]

One thing remains missing, however. The process as it has been described so far could be a purely domestic one and is in no way necessarily

---

[28] In that respect one is reminded of Schelling's classic theories of nuclear deterrence and the idea of automatizing the decision to order certain nuclear counter-strikes as a means of convincing the adversary that a decision to retaliate by nuclear means is not an option. T.C. Schelling, *The Strategy of Conflict* (Cambridge MA, Harvard University Press 1960).

or recognizably international. A first specificity of the ICC *vis-à-vis* purely national constitutionalization is that it aims to anchor that intertemporal commitment internationally.

2.2 Internationalization: complementarity as the 'international anchoring of an intertemporal commitment'

Although interested in the formation of constitutions and the deeper logical problems they raise, Elster is not particularly interested in some of the key weaknesses of constitutions and, most relevantly for our purposes, how these can be remedied by resorting to international means. The problem with merely domestic constitutional precommitments, as history has shown, is that they can be wrecked relatively easily. A constitution is nothing more than an agreement between the sovereign and itself, to be undone once the sovereign musters enough resolve to do so, by force if need be. The constitutional promise that lacks a higher ally that would stand behind it in cases of exception, therefore, can be of little impact.

In the myth of Ulysses and the sirens, Ulysses' bounds were of the kind that he could not possibly untie himself. But it is difficult to find constitutional analogues that would not allow for at least some considerable leeway in the face of a massive reaffirmation of the actuality of the sovereign's power. If a government emerges that is willing to trample constitutional guarantees and to harness the violence of the State to overcome their constraints, then the constitution may be a paper-thin protection. Tomorrow's sovereign may relatively easily decide to renege on the promises of his earlier incarnation. Hence we know perfectly well that, following periods when international crimes were committed, unconstitutional amnesties and pardons were proclaimed with little chance for victims to protest (or not until a few decades later).

Hence we arrive at the idea of anchoring a domestic commitment to certain norms internationally, and therefore combining the logic of precommitment with that of internationalization. Indeed, it is surprising that until two very recent articles by Steven Ratner[29] and Andrew Moravcsik,[30]

---

[29] S.R. Ratner, 'Overcoming Temptations to Violate Human Dignity in Times of Crisis: On the Possibilities for Meaningful Self-Restraint', 5 *Theoretical Inquiries in Law* (2004), 33 <http://ssrn.com/abstract=405401> (7 July 2005) ('Herein lies the role for externally

the former in the context of humanitarian obligations and the latter in relation to international human rights courts, no one seemed to have thought of linking these two powerful ideas together.

Subscribing to international obligations that reinforce and legitimize domestic obligations can be seen as a way of reinforcing domestic commitments by tying them up in a web of interstate obligations. An up-to-then purely internal promise is taken out of the realm of the domestic and into that of the collective. The logic of such a 'collectivization' of what would otherwise have been a series of isolated commitments is that it reinforces the strength of each participant's resolve by creating what I would call an 'international community of commitment'.[31]

The classic locus for such international experiments has of course been the international protection of human rights, with which international criminal law bears many similarities. Each State Party to international human rights agreements manifests its intent to be bound by certain international human rights norms. In joining such a set-up, each State gains the right to participate in the institutions that are created as a result and to inquire about the human rights behaviour of other States (through interstate complaints mechanisms in particular).

The State, however, is in return prevented from claiming that his sovereignty is being interfered with when other States do the same. Concern for human rights is, in a sense, collectivized. In normal times, the international

---

imposed constraints, which can complement the internal strategies.'). Ratner then compares Elsterian precommitment theory and IR approaches to incentives by international organizations. See also J.A. Roberston, "Paying the Alligator': Precommitment in Law, Bioethics, and Constitutions', 81 *Texas L Rev* (2003), 1729, 1744 ('International organizations built through the voluntary participation of sovereign nations might also be thought of as a form of precommitment by nation-states seeking to restrain the future action of other states by agreeing to restrain their own actions.'). However, Robertson's reference to 'other states' is troubling because it is not clear what relation it bears to precommitment.

[30] Interestingly, Moravcsik anticipates that '[t]he logic of 'locking in' credible domestic policies through international commitments can be generalized to other human rights regimes – including the recent International Criminal Court ...'. Moravcsik (n. 1) 220.

[31] On ratification of international human rights treaties, Ratner has said that the treaty's 'form as a promise to *other* states does not per se make it any less of a precommitment.' Ratner (n. 29) 13. I would go further: A precommitment mediated by an international agreement is even more of a precommitment than one that is not so mediated because it provides a powerful added incentive to comply with the precommitment.

community ensures that States adhere to best international practices. In exceptional times, when the temptation to do away with rights arises, the international community acts as an ultimate guarantor of a rights culture.

Essentially, what the State does when it joins such a set-up is it to make it difficult for itself to turn back on its commitments by making the international community formally witness that commitment, increasing at least the 'embarrassment' cost of having to renege on publicly made promises.[32] What would otherwise have been considered a purely internal matter becomes international because the default of any individual participant will weaken the overall set-up. Impunity in one country will encourage impunity in other countries unless the problem can be effectively contained and dealt with by the ICC. This makes it difficult for any State to claim that its eventual change of mind is its decision and its decision alone because it is the only one affected.

Although very little of the huge literature on the ICC has given any attention to this key point, the ICC can be seen as part of a very similar process of internationalization of a precommitment. In ratifying the Rome Statute, the State is effectively affirming to the international community its commitment to carry out domestic prosecutions. It is asking the international community to take its word seriously on that point and even to intervene against it in case of default. It is therefore prospectively legitimizing the international community's intervention into what would have otherwise been considered internal matters by flagging the issue of how to deal with international crimes as one that is no longer purely internal.

If we return to the Ulysses metaphor, one could argue that fellow States Parties are to any other State Party tempted by the sirens of impunity what the sailors are to Ulysses. A State Party can no longer make up its mind as it goes about how to deal with international crimes: Even if it wanted not to be bound by its previous decision to try them, even if it sought to invoke special circumstances or a radical change of mind, other States would have all the legitimacy in the world – the State's own sovereign mandate – to protect it against itself, to protect it against the sirens of impunity. The only

---

[32] This is the equivalent of Elster's mention of 'audience effects' as one of the devices through which commitments are maintained. See J. Elster, *Ulysses Unbound: Studies in Rationality, Precommitment, and Constraints* (Cambridge, Cambridge University Press 2000) 69.

added complexity, of course, is that everyone on the ICC boat is called to play both the part of a sailor and the part of Ulysses, depending on the circumstances, so that the ICC involves a much more communal and non-hierarchic element than Homer's tale and Elster's interpretation of it.

There are two ways of specifying what calculations lie behind such a move that replicate the distinction we identified in the previous section between joining the ICC as essentially one government binding successor governments or as a government binding itself. One is to say that what a government does when it joins the ICC is it uses the continuity of the State to bind other governments in the future. As Andrew Moravcsik put it, governments resort to international bodies to 'reduc[e] political uncertainty'[33] and to 'constrain the behavior of future national governments'[34] by '"lock[ing] in" favored policies ..., thereby insulating them from the actions of future governments.'[35] In fact, Andrew Moravcsik sees the internationalization of human rights precommitments precisely as a way of reinforcing their intertemporal reach: '[G]overnments turn to international enforcement when an international commitment effectively enforces the policy preferences of a particular government at a particular point in time against future domestic political alternatives.'[36] The goal is none other than to tie the hand of future governments:

> 'By placing interpretation in the hands of independent authorities managed in part by foreign governments – in other words, by alienating sovereignty to an international body – governments seek to establish reliable judicial constraints on future non-democratic governments or on democratically elected governments that may seek ... to subvert democracy from within.'[37]

Again, however, as in our exploration of constitutional precommitment, things are always a little more complicated than a government simply binding another government. In a sense, it is not only 'the State that is binding itself' (although, as we have seen, that may essentially be a formal notion) but also that it may well be that, through that device, a particular govern-

---

[33] Moravcsik (n. 1) 228.
[34] Ibid.
[35] Ibid.
[36] Ibid. 220.
[37] Ibid. 228.

ment binds itself against its own potential future shortcomings. The point is that internationalization also makes powerful sense in this case because governments can feel that the international community is a valid last recourse if they ever stray too far away from their own once expressed commitments. The logic of precommitment of an actor by itself permeates the emergence of the ICC through and through.

2.3   Institutionalization: the specificity of complementarity as the transfer of State functions to an international body

It is trite to say that international promises not backed by appropriate institutional means can be mere rhetoric. We recognize strong normative regimes as those that are backed by appropriate and functional institutions.[38] Having said this, the ICC of course represents a highly specific type of institutionalization, not only in general but also in relation to other modes of international institutionalization. In this section I examine the peculiarity of the ICC and complementarity as an institutional/judicial solution to the problem of impunity. I therefore begin by highlighting the institutionalization methods of the closest analogue to the international criminal law

---

[38] The combination of precommitment, 'going public' (i.e., going international in the context of States joining the ICC), and institutionalization can here be illustrated by an analogy with the often used example of marriage. See, e.g., J. Elster, *Sour Grapes: Studies in the Subversion of Rationality* (Cambridge, Cambridge University Press 1983) 114-15: First, through marriage, two persons who are in love at the time of getting married commit themselves to staying together, for better or for worse. We (and they) of course know that their love may not last forever. However, by linking their fates through the institution of marriage, the bride and groom attempt precisely to ensure themselves against reversals in passion through a commitment, expressed in the present, to spend the rest of their lives together. Therefore, marriage falls typically within the logic of long-term precommitment. The force of that initial promise is supposed to make going through the ups and downs of life easier and to make a separation at least marginally more difficult. Second, the spouses make their community a witness to that commitment. To the extent that the spouses' identities and interests are shaped by the community, the decision to 'go public' amounts to a substantial incentive to keep the marriage together. The communalization of an individual decision ensures that a decision to default on marriage vows is taken away from the strictly individual and may involve family, community and social consequences. Third, the institutional dimension is provided by the fact that the spouses essentially contract into an entire institutional and legal machinery that raises the costs of walking out of a relationship (divorce rather than simple factual separation).

regime – international human rights law – and show how the ICC differs markedly from any previously existing arrangement.

2.3.1   *The international human rights courts model*

International human rights courts, the closest antecedent to the ICC, have all been based on the traditional sanction mechanism of the international legal order, State responsibility. The problem of systematically and effectively engaging State responsibility in a general forum such as the International Court of Justice (ICJ), which States may be reluctant to join because the wide range of cases that might be litigated before it creates unpredictability, is avoided in the case of human rights courts by the creation of a specialized sub-regime in which States, generally in a regional context, are more willing to submit to compulsory jurisdiction. The result, and quite a remarkable one at that, is that State responsibility, perhaps the most fundamental institution of classical international law, remained the indispensable mediator between international concern and domestic harm in a field as remote from classical international law as human rights.

The ICC regime is more complex and also more revolutionary. As is obvious, failure by a State to prosecute international crimes does not involve, in the context of the ICC, any finding of State responsibility. (It is, however, an interesting sub-debate in itself whether a finding by the ICC that a State has been 'unwilling or unable' to prosecute international crimes might be used to establish State responsibility elsewhere.) Instead, the sanction (or at least a consequence because, strictly speaking, it is not a sanction) for a State which has failed to prosecute is that the repression of the crime in question may be handed over to the ICC.

There is, in other words, a *disintermediation* of the process of sanctioning violations of international norms. Instead of going through State responsibility and obliging the State to live up to its obligations to repress international crimes, the consequence of a default is that the ICC steps in to exercise the relevant sovereign function (criminal repression) in lieu of the State. A State failure makes the State, in a sense, transparent; it deprives it momentarily of its monopoly of jurisdiction, allowing the ICC to step into its shoes. The State is considered unworthy of its sovereign prerogative which is then exercised internationally.

2.3.2   *The road not taken: an ICC based on the same model*

In theory, it is worth insisting that there is no reason why the ICC could not
have been a court shaped on the model of human rights courts. The Court
could have been a 'specialised ICJ', an 'International Court of Criminal
Justice', that would have had as its specific subject-matter States' obligations in matters of international criminal law. In other words, the ICC could
have been to international criminal law what the International Tribunal on
the Law of the Sea is to the law of the sea or World Trade Organization
panels are to the law of international trade: a reasonably robust, State re-
sponsibility-based mechanism for ensuring that States stick to their international criminal law obligations (essentially *aut dedere aut judicare*
provisions).

However, the impatience with international crimes was such that this
possibility was hardly contemplated. The reasoning seems to have been
that one could not possibly wait for States to bring cases before such an
international judicial body. It is true that State reluctance to bring cases
against fellow States when no matter of pressing national interest is involved is well known (and, to the extent that the crimes were committed
purely internally, that may well often be the case). After all, no State has
ever brought a case before the ICJ in all its history to try to engage a State's
responsibility for failure to prosecute: Why would States do so now?

That opposition, however, does not seem conclusive, and a way of sal-
vaging State responsibility as a sanction mechanism while avoiding the risk
of State inertia in initiating cases would have been conceivable. Rather than
waiting for States to bring cases and in view of the *erga omnes* and collective nature of the obligations involved, an international prosecutor could
have been entrusted to sue States systematically for their failures to prosecute international crimes, ensuring both systematicity and even-handed-
ness. Nor is it inconceivable that States would have agreed to such a regime.
Is not a finding that a State has been 'unwilling or unable' to exercise its
responsibilities, if not analytically at least symbolically, just as damning?

2.3.3   *Why not State responsibility?*

So why the aspiration – indeed, the urge – to bypass State responsibility
altogether? Essentially, the decision to make the ICC into an 'international

criminal court of substitution' seems to have been premised on a profound distrust of State responsibility, even if that responsibility could have been engaged more systematically. State responsibility was probably always perceived as too cumbersome and indirect a means, compared to swift prosecutions of individuals suspected of international crimes by an international criminal tribunal. This is not unreasonable. State responsibility may take a long time to be established. Once the harm of impunity is done, it may take a great deal longer to correct it, while it is understood that criminal justice, especially in the case of grave international crimes, should proceed relatively expeditiously. This option, moreover, may have also been States' implicitly preferred outcome because they still favoured, all other things being equal, a procedural finding that they were 'unwilling or unable' to a substantive finding that they were in violation of an international obligation to prosecute.

The ultimate shape that the ICC took is also a function of its intellectual history. Despite all the talk about complementarity and the centrality that this idea has ended up taking in the context of the Court, the idea was always to create an international criminal tribunal. It was never *per se* to find ways to ensure that national courts would be up to the standards expected of them. Diplomats and scholars were discussing the idea of an international criminal court long before they even had given the slightest attention to the issue of relations with national jurisdictions. Had the starting-point been the need to find better ways to force domestic jurisdictions to do their work properly, it may well be that an interstate responsibility mechanism would have been favoured. But the fact that the starting-point was always the need to have an international criminal tribunal meant that the option of a State responsibility mechanism was never even really debated.

2.3.4   *The consequences of that choice*

Whatever the reasons for that choice, it is worth noting the relative distrust in the institutions of the State that the ICC evidences, notwithstanding complementarity. Human rights courts, by relying on the State to correct situations prejudicial to human rights, invested a certain faith in the State's capacity to make good its shortcomings. On the contrary, the ICC regime suggests that a State which is found at one point to be 'unwilling or unable' to try certain crimes is, essentially, beyond redemption, that, in other words, engaging its responsibility and ordering it to comply with its obligations would be inadequate or even inappropriate in view of the stakes. Indeed, complementarity does not, for example, even afford the State a second chance. The process whereby a case will be transferred from the national to the international is a one-off, final one, insusceptible to any changes in the relevant States' attitudes.

One result is that the ICC regime represents a reality that is substantially more integrated with the domestic legal system than in the human rights model and, in fact, than any previously existing model of international enforcement. International human rights bodies were still very much external to the domestic system, however much they sought to constrain it through the State. The ICC, on the contrary, will act as a direct substitute for national jurisdictions. Not only does it represent a much more forceful incursion into and displacement of sovereignty, but it also suggests an affinity between the international and the national that was previously unknown.

If constitutionalization reflected the basic reasoning behind ensuring oneself against the temptation of impunity and internationalization the fact that this commitment is collectivized, then institutionalization points to the actual strength of the ties that bind the sovereign. For Ulysses, simply being scolded for not resisting the sirens would not have been enough since, quite simply, not resisting the calls of the sirens would have meant his demise. Similarly, presumably because ICC States Parties consider that failure to repress international crimes is something particularly grave (graver, for instance, than failing to honour a standard international human rights obligation), they seek to bind themselves with ties that make their precommitment particularly constraining. The idea is not to leave open even the option of simply defaulting and then having to pay some comparatively minor price (as would have been the case with State responsibility). In the case of the ICC, there is no interest in defaulting since that would lead to a clearly worse outcome than what a State could bring about if it abided by its own precommitment (not only will the individuals be tried anyhow in the case of failure of national jurisdictions, but they will be tried by an international criminal court rather than the State's own legal system).

In the section that follows, I try to come up with an overall theory of how the ICC's solution to enforcement is a particularly strong one and how it ties up nicely with the notion of precommitment.

2.4   The coming into existence and precise nature of complementarity: an analysis

We have seen so far what the specificity of complementarity is in relation to traditional human rights mechanisms: a system of remedying international breaches that substitutes an international system of criminal repression for a national one instead of using the medium of State responsibility. There remain some oddities, however. What will the exact nature of the jurisdiction exercised by the Court be in each case? How did it come about? What is so special about it?

It seems important in this context to explore some more doctrinal aspects of the Rome Statute's logic to see if the elements we have come up with so far are vindicated by any reading of the relevant provisions. Many commentators discuss the Court's jurisdiction as an institutional problem. What exactly the Court's jurisdiction covers may be an interesting debate in its own right, but it does not really tell us anything about the fundamental nature of that jurisdiction or how it came about.

Rather than talk about the Court's jurisdiction, which is presumably simply conferred to it by the Rome Statute as far as the Court is concerned, I want to investigate the issue of what *titles* to jurisdiction the Court is actually exercising when it tries individuals accused of the core international crimes. The issue of titles to jurisdiction is of course one of the oldest and most venerable questions of international law, but it is one traditionally confined to our understanding of the State. Nonetheless, it makes sense to talk in terms of titles to jurisdiction in the case of the ICC, particularly because the Court's jurisdiction deals with matters so similar to those traditionally taken care of by the State.

What titles to jurisdiction will the Court use when it exercises its jurisdiction? The provision referring to pre-conditions for the exercise of jurisdiction is the closest equivalent to a clause determining the Court's jurisdiction *ratione loci*. According to Article 12, paragraph 2, of the Rome Statute, except in cases of referral by the United Nations Security Council, the ICC 'may exercise its jurisdiction'[39] in cases where '[t]he State on the territory of which the conduct in question occurred'[40] or '[t]he State of

---

[39] Rome Statute (n. 11) Art. 12 para. 2.
[40] Ibid. Art. 12 para. 2a.

which the person accused of the crime is a national'[41] is a State Party. One interpretation, therefore, might be that the Court effectively has imperfect territorial and personal titles to jurisdiction, at least to the extent that, for the ICC to exercise jurisdiction, it must be proven that the national judicial system has not worked properly.

I do not believe, however, that this is the right explanation. The Court does not have territorial or personal titles to jurisdiction because the Court does not have a territory or nationals. The Court might have 'a jurisdiction' that has to be interpreted in light of the principles of territory and nationality, but not the corresponding 'titles to jurisdiction'.

The better view is that the titles to jurisdiction are and remain fundamentally the State's but that they are transferred to the ICC, which is occasionally called upon to exercise them in lieu of and on behalf of the State. This is an interesting perspective from the point of view of complementarity. It means that the ICC's real title to jurisdiction is a process of delegation whereby States entrust titles to jurisdiction to the Court. What converts these titles from imperfect to perfect ones is the failure of national jurisdictions.[42]

Admissibility is of course presented in the ICC Statute essentially as a procedural issue. But admissibility is in fact also a deeply jurisdictional issue in its own right. The question of the malfunctioning of domestic jurisdictions is, in a sense, no less jurisdictional than the Court's jurisdiction *ratione materiae, ratione loci* or *ratione temporis*.[43] The Court's jurisdic-

---

[41] Ibid. Art. 12 para. 2b.

[42] Even in the context of the *ad hoc* tribunals, the absence of a complementarity requirement giving the Tribunals apparently unlimited discretion to prosecute did not mean that they effectively had territorial and personal titles to jurisdiction exercisable against the former Yugoslavia and Rwanda. In that case, I would argue that the title to the courts' jurisdiction lay in the identification by the Security Council of a threat to international peace and security and the regime of primacy as an exceptional regime of derogation.

[43] During the process leading to the Rome Conference, issues of complementarity were in fact sometimes referred to as issues of jurisdiction and sometimes as issues of admissibility. The only reason I can think of for classifying them under different headings is that while, say, the commission of the crime of genocide on the territory of a State Party after the date of that State Party's ratification of the Statute is a relatively raw fact, the determination of a dysfunctional domestic court is something that has to be evaluated on a case-by-case basis and that, as a result, requires a sophisticated procedural machinery. In addition, there is a

tion, if we take the word jurisdiction seriously as 'what the Court has competence for', might just as well be reformulated as 'jurisdiction over these crimes committed in the territory of States Parties that have been inadequately prosecuted'. In fact, the suggestion here is that the ICC's ultimate title to jurisdiction in any given case is none other than the failure of domestic jurisdictions over crimes committed on the territory or by the nationals of States Parties.

How does that process of delegation come about? This is where we can begin to wrap up preceding developments and ascertain their overall meaning.

There are essentially two ways of looking at the matter. The first is that the Rome Statute creates a system in which the failure of a national jurisdiction essentially means that the territorial or national title to jurisdiction is transferred to the ICC on a case-by-case basis. In other words, up and until the moment that admissibility is established, the ICC has no claim whatsoever to jurisdiction; the transfer of title is effectuated at the moment when the failure is formally identified.

Another and perhaps more sophisticated way of looking at things is that the jurisdictional title was always virtually the ICC's from the moment the relevant State ratified the Rome Statute. When ratifying the Statute, a State Party transfers a virtual or imperfect title to jurisdiction to the Court. This the State does as a sort of guarantee of its good faith, a little in the way that one would place collateral to secure a loan.[44] In monetary terms, one could say that States' titles to jurisdiction are like the gold deposits in a central bank devoted to upholding the credibility of a currency: a guarantee that the value and credibility of a national judiciary is backed by a commitment to sustain that value and credibility. Here the ICC acts as a repressor of last resort.

The Court then holds on to that title, bound not to use it unless the State reneges on its promise. If the State complies with its international obligations, then nothing comes out of that initial transfer; in case of default,

---

desire that the Prosecutor feel free to investigate these cases on account of their intrinsic value, without being hampered initially by the issue of whether domestic courts are functioning.

[44] If one wants to weave that metaphor further, the loan can be interpreted here as the added credibility that participation in the ICC regime lends to the participating State.

however, the international community, through the ICC, has an option to recoup that title and exercise it. The system sends a strong signal to all participating States about the solidity of an inter-subjective commitment backed by credible supranational enforcement.

The analogy has its limits but this admittedly formalistic reading none-theless seems vindicated by the Statute and would make sense of the appar-ently formal jurisdiction/admissibility distinction. Indeed, the Statute does seem to suggest that the Court has the virtual exercise of a delegated title to jurisdiction over the territory and nationals of States Parties all along and that all that is needed to make that jurisdiction 'real' is for a given case to be considered admissible.

3.   CONCLUSION: CONSTITUTIONALIZATION AND BEYOND …

We have seen that it was very improbable that States would join the ICC if they saw such a step as potentially incompatible with their national interest. We then saw that the risk was precisely that the only States that would join would be States whose obvious national interest it was to join, in other words, States that had nothing to fear from the ICC. In such a situation, the ICC would have had very little to do indeed. Our appreciation of the ICC and its chances of doing anything meaningful in the world thus seems to hinge on our capacity to come up with a theory of why States that would be reasonably likely to commit international crimes entering the Court's juris-diction might nonetheless want to ratify the Rome Statute.

I have sought to provide exactly such a theory in the form of a 'best possible scenario' of why States might join the ICC in a reasonably self-interested yet reasonably enlightened way that goes beyond strict realism but does not ask us to embrace some wild claim about States sacrificing their sovereignty for the global good. I have suggested that, interpreted in the right light, complementarity can provide the key to that normative puzzle. In joining the ICC, States can arguably be seen as protecting themselves against their own risk of defaulting from their once expressed commitment to rein in impunity. Rather than just do this domestically, they enlist the assistance of an international institution to increase the cost of default. The peculiarity of the ICC as an international mechanism lies in the fact that, unlike international human rights courts, it foregoes State responsibility as a sanction mechanism. Instead, through complementarity, the State essentially gives the ICC a mandate to act in its place in case of failure. The doctrinal reconstruction of this succession of moves suggests that they can be stylized as the transfer of imperfect titles to jurisdiction to the ICC, to be exercised by it in case the State is not up to its obligations.

As Steven Ratner put it:

'[S]tates ... face ... situations where observance of the law does not, in the eyes of many, seem in its best interests. The key to promoting the law in these scenarios is to set up a dynamic whereby the state sees the law as more than some unrealistic piece of moral advice.'[45]

If the ICC is ever to become a powerful and meaningful Court, complementarity thus seems to be the only device, and an unprecedented one, that can raise the prospects of that happening. But what does precommitment theory reveal and indeed does it reveal anything?[46]

One way of seeing the contribution of precommitment theory is as an explanation of what at least some States might or must be doing. Whether any hesitantly virtuous State actually thinks in the way I have suggested is of course anybody's guess at this stage and would have to await empirical validation. Unfortunately, it is unlikely that States would be very explicit internationally about such reasoning since it does involve a rather paradoxical admission of potential weakness. Most States that join the Court are thus likely to present themselves as the kind that joins because it has nothing to fear from the Court.

---

[45] Ratner (n. 29) 35.

[46] One of the true sources of ambiguity surrounding precommitment theory is truly what it is about. In that respect, attempts to apply precommitment reasoning to the international realm are often hesitant about what they are doing and particularly about whether the emphasis on precommitment reasoning is (1) an explanation of what States actually do, (2) an argument about what States should do, (3) an idea about how States might think of what it is they do, (4) an exploration of whether the compliance record of States that have indisputably entered on the basis of precommitment reasoning might be different from that of other States (and, if so, how). I understand Ratner, for example, as doing the first: '[S]ome states presumably enter into treaties on human dignity because they really do wish to tie their hands'. Ibid. 13. I also understand him as doing the fourth: Precommitment theory 'can help understand better the conditions under which [States having entered a treaty on the basis of precommitment reasoning] will be tempted to violate those commitments.' Ibid. 15. To an extent he also does the second and the third by suggesting that '[t]he prescriptions in this essay require implementation by elites and the public'. Ibid. 36.

Perhaps the point of highlighting such a seemingly sophisticated set of reasons why States would want to join the Court is to show by its absurdity how very few are likely to do so. It may be indeed that no State thinks in these terms at all, in which case it will turn out that those hesitantly virtuous States that have joined have joined merely because the prospect of a new loan or trade agreement with the EU was simply too irresistible or because a parliamentary assembly late in the night thought that this one on a long list of international commitments was one they simply could not avoid. The danger here is that, with the depth of actual commitment to international criminal justice running low, the Court's legitimacy will be challenged when it effectively exercises jurisdiction, as these States reassess their national interest in light of changing circumstances.

My impression, however, is that, although actual precommitment may be unusual, the reasoning that I have outlined, in addition to being a requirement of strong commitment to the Court, must at least be present in infinitesimal traces in the back of some statesmen's heads when they decide to take their States into the ICC. It makes sense that States joining the ICC with a reasonably likely prospect of having some of their nationals as candidates for prosecution should at least be able to tie that move to some discrete domestic goal. It is not entirely utopian that some States, particularly weak States with a chequered record of dealing with traumatic episodes involving the commission of international crimes, should seek to enlist preventively the assistance of the international community to deal with some of their intractable problems of impunity. It is worth remembering that in the early 1990s it was precisely out of fear that their national courts would not be up to the task of dealing with narcotics trafficking crimes that a number of Caribbean States had asked the United Nations General Assembly to reconsider the creation of an international criminal court. Rwanda itself asked for the creation of the International Criminal Tribunal for Rwanda, among other reasons, because it must have thought that an international criminal tribunal would assist it in its task. There is more plausibility to this idea than catches the attention of many of the bigger and more powerful States, who typically conceive of the ICC in terms of a net loss of sovereignty rather than as an occasional de-multiplier of it.

Another slightly different way of looking at the added value of precommitment theory is more normative and constructivist in nature. It may be that simply uncovering and detailing this complex normative route to the ICC is something that can help sustain certain narratives of why States would want to join the Court. Although ICC enthusiasts are not generally at want for words, I have often been struck by their unease, often a result of ultra-principled human rights backgrounds, with the language of State interest. I have always thought that calls to States that they simply 'join the ICC', because such is now the way of international justice, simply fail to take the national interest seriously and answer the question, 'Why would one?'. The capacity to come up with a reasonably elaborate answer to that question is crucial, it seems to me, to enrich our normative vocabulary and our understanding, if not of why States have already joined the Court, then of why they might nonetheless consider doing so in a way that is reasonably grounded in the reality of international experience. To the extent that civil society can master a discourse such as the one I have outlined, some of what at times seems like an unbridgeable divide between State interest and civil society's idealism may occasionally be bridged. In the best of worlds, States might actually end up precommitting largely because they are enlightened about the fact that this is indeed an available option.[47]

At any rate, if some States are indeed joining the ICC for reasons that essentially or partly have to do with precommitment, then there may be lessons to heed in terms of these States' compliance with the Rome Statute. The fact that a State joined the ICC with such reasoning in mind will make it more difficult for a subsequent government confronted with an attempt by the Court to assert its jurisdiction to describe that assertion as fundamentally illegitimate. That the decision to be bound was taken by a previous government with what seem to be substantially different preferences will be precisely the point, and certainly not a valid excuse to default (certainly not in law but also not in terms of legitimacy). On the contrary, the international community will be able to present itself – helpfully, one would think – as the ally of that State's better understood and long-term interest as once expressed by the State itself.

---

[47] This might be seen as a sort of functional equivalent to what Ratner describes as 'inducing passion' by showing States how joining the ICC need not be conceived of as a net loss in terms of national interest even when they are at risk of committing international crimes but can be seen as simply another way of thinking of the national interest. Ratner (n. 29) 26, 31.

In the rest of this conclusion and as a sort of postscript, I want to think a little more prospectively in order to examine how that overall set-up might solidify into something very different in the future. All the preceding developments focus on States' decisions to join the ICC at the moment that they decide to join. It does not seem superfluous, however, to remember that the original motivations for joining the Court will probably soon recede into the background and to explore how the ICC will, in all likelihood, take on a life of its own irrespective of whatever projections States made onto it at the moment of joining. Otherwise the risk is that our vision of the ICC will be dominated by the circumstances of the Court's creation rather than a vision of the reality that its very existence might create. The international order after the ICC will – although perhaps sometimes only in subtle ways – be different from the one that gave rise to it so that, as time passes, States' motivations for joining may also evolve.

Our vision so far has taken the State very much as its starting-point; it has, in other words, been a bottom-up vision, seeing the ICC's potential power to supersede domestic jurisdiction as something that is very much granted by and therefore dependent on the State. That is probably a good description of how the ICC and complementarity came about, but it is also probable that, once the ICC has stabilized into a durable institution, some of that coming-into-being will recede into the background. The ICC itself will contribute to changing our understanding of sovereignty.

In the previous reasoning, the State was very much transferring a title to jurisdiction to the international community. But what if that title to jurisdiction had never been entirely the State's to dispose of and instead had always been, in a certain sense, granted to it by the international community in the first place? Surely, if that were the case, then the international community would merely be claiming back what had always belonged to it.

I am reminded in this context of the old debate on the origin and nature of sovereignty and international law and the classic chicken-and-egg problem of knowing whether international law came before sovereignty or the other way around. In the vision that we have outlined so far, titles to jurisdiction merely derive from the existence of sovereignty, with the discretion to be then vested in an institution such as the ICC. This replicates the old voluntarist idea that all international law is sovereign-created. Sovereignty is, in a sense, both its own definition and ontologically prior to all of its commitments.

Another and quite opposite vision would be that international law is indeed logically prior to the existence of sovereignty, that the content of sovereignty is itself defined by international law. The idea here is that sovereignty is in fact defined by its proper usage and, in particular, the obligation to use it in a way that does not offend the international community, for example by allowing crimes committed on its territory or by its nationals to go unpunished. Surely, even if sovereignty was hardly always defined as such, there would be a case that it is nowadays.

But perhaps yet another (and probably more convincing) vision is that sovereignty and international law are mutually constituted. There is no 'sovereignty outside international law' anymore than there is 'international law outside sovereignty'. One of the things this probably implies is that, although titles to criminal jurisdiction have always been there for the sovereign to use, the nature of these titles and their proper usage was in fact all along determined by international law. In fact, the State's titles to jurisdiction were in a sense always conferred by international law. There is no territorial or personal title to jurisdiction of the sovereign State in the absolute; the legitimacy of these titles is conditional upon their recognition by international law (albeit, admittedly, a very sovereign-oriented international law).

This is not simply out of some a-historical, ontological sense *a priori* in favour of the analytical priority of international law. Were that precedence not the case, the free and unhindered use of titles to jurisdiction by the State could not occur and would, among other things, be marred by perpetual conflicts of jurisdiction. It is not a coincidence that one of the first and most important decisions of the then newly created Permanent Court of International Justice was the famous *Lotus* case.[48] The consequence of a State having those titles to jurisdiction is that the State has these and only these titles; international law, in that respect, fulfils an irreplaceable coordination role.

If we see the content and proper use of the State's titles to jurisdiction as being fundamentally defined by international law, then we have to be open to the possibility that this proper use will evolve in time with international norms. The predominant vision of titles to jurisdiction has traditionally been

---

[48] *Case of the S.S. 'Lotus' (France v. Turkey), PCIJ Rep Series* A No. 10 (1927).

that, once the State's, these are essentially in the order of a prerogative. Jurisdiction is the privilege of the sovereign, one that he may use at his discretion.

If we re-contextualize the idea of titles to jurisdiction into contemporary debates on the evolving nature of sovereignty, however, it should become clear that the recognition by international law of some of the State's titles to jurisdiction now comes, in the case of international crimes, with strings attached, namely the obligation to use them to keep a check on impunity. In this would-be 'post-impunity age', the decision whether or not to prosecute has been taken out of the realm of sovereign discretion (in fact, whether or not States join the ICC). From there to saying that the recognition of titles to jurisdiction in such cases is conditional upon their proper exercise, there is only a small step.

The closest analogy here is ongoing discussions on the nature of sovereignty in the context of humanitarian intervention. Although of course deeply contentious (and I am not interested here in taking sides on this debate as much as showing its affinity with the present), one of the ideas to emerge is a broad vision of sovereignty as generally conditional upon its proper exercise, which is understood as an exercise that conforms with certain fundamental standards of humanity. Failure to conform to such standards may expose the State to a breach of its sovereignty by the international community seeking to correct a wrong done to the population.

Complementarity is the sector-specific, sovereign-sanctioned device by which that vision of sovereignty is actualized in the field of international criminal law. The deeper reasoning underlying such a move seems to be the one that lies behind human rights and international criminal justice in general: International crimes have simply become too grave a matter ever to be considered purely internal even when they lack any trans- or multinational elements. Complementarity is less contentious than an overall vision of sovereignty as conditional precisely because it is sector-specific, with international criminal law being perhaps the one field in which a sizeable proportion of the international community is ready to move ahead with a more vigorous concept of international control of sovereign prerogatives. It is nonetheless a significant step in a direction that remains by and large deeply contentious, as shown by the more general debate on humanitarian intervention, for example, but also by the fact that, even within an issue-based regime such as international criminal law, many States have decided not to join the Court.

The vision of sovereignty that emerges as a result is by no means an 'emasculated' one; sovereignty can be reasonably confident in its capacity to remain the basic building block of the international legal order. Complementarity should at least, on one account, reinforce it in that vision: After all, the State still gets the first shot at launching prosecutions for international crimes, an explicit recognition that international crimes will almost always be committed in practice against a given State's legal order and that this State will be the best place to sanction them.

But a deep sense of the precariousness of that first-go, of the State's exclusivity in matters criminal also emerges. Although how precarious the State's hold on its criminal power is will have to await more substantial definition of the 'unwilling or unable' threshold, the very possibility that a State risks being deprived of a case because of its inadequate handling of it is almost revolutionary. The State becomes merely the first rung of a ladder, a localized outpost of the international legal order's now increasingly centralized organs of criminal repression. It is no longer an autonomous agent of *dédoublement fonctionnel*, but the supervised enforcer of an integrated global regime for the repression of international crimes.

If we see things in that very different light, we can start understanding that the emergence of a complementarity-based ICC is part of the international community's own process of constitutionalization and self-realization. Once the initial foundational steps of the ICC have been adopted, whether the title to jurisdiction is one entrusted to the ICC by the sovereign State or one entrusted to the sovereign State by the ICC are two issues that become virtually indistinguishable. In other words, beyond the conditions of its creation, the ICC will become the embodiment of the idea that sovereignty is a much less untrammelled and absolute power, as a considerable power that is nonetheless thoroughly constrained by international law and whose continuous self-exercise remains profoundly conditional on respecting certain fundamental international prescriptions.

Chapter 2
SOVEREIGNTY IN THE DOCK

*Gerben Kor**

> Nothing exists except atoms and empty space.
> *All the rest is opinion.*
> (Democritus of Abdera).

1. THE *DORAN* CASE

Doran is a native of Overland. In 2006 there was a civil war in Overland. After the war, Overland was divided into Minorland and Majorland. Doran was a politician on the side of Minorland and is now imprisoned in Majorland. He is, by his own account, a national of Minorland. He is accused of crimes against humanity and will be transferred to the International Criminal Court. His alleged crimes have taken place on the territory of what is now Minorland and on the territory of what is now Majorland. Overland was not a State Party to the Rome Statute. Majorland is a State Party; Minorland is not.

2. INTRODUCTION

In this chapter I explore the conceptual relationship between the individual and sovereignty in light of the complementarity principle of the International Criminal Court (ICC). The impact of the complementarity principle of the ICC on the (judicial) sovereignty of States has been the subject of much political and legal debate. The position of the individual has often been neglected in that debate. This chapter gives a central position to the

* Ph.D. candidate in Philosophy of Law, Free University of Amsterdam.

J.K. Kleffner & G. Kor (eds.), Complementary Views on Complementarity
© 2006, T·M·C·ASSER PRESS, *The Hague, The Netherlands and the Authors*

individual, or to be more precise, to the accused – the position of the victim will not be discussed. In section 3 I present a concept of the individual. Section 4 deals with sovereignty. In sections 5 and 6, the notions of world order and international criminal law are discussed. Section 7 deals with complementarity and its bearing on the relationship between the individual and sovereignty.

The reader will find that there are many simplifications in this chapter. That is done on purpose; I believe in the power of simplification when it comes to analysing legal – and political – issues. Of course I realize that a simplification cannot be the *terminus* of a legal inquiry, but it may help to clear the tracks that lie before us.

3.   THE INDIVIDUAL

In this chapter 'the individual' is defined as a person, a human being, possibly a bearer of rights and duties. An individual is by no means defined in the same sense all around the world. For the sake of this chapter, it is not all that relevant if one holds a liberal, communist, Aristotelian, Nietzschian, religious, Eastern, Western, Northern, or Southern view of the concept of the individual. I try to strip the individual of all of those connotations and to look at his naked existence. Every human being with a pulse is an individual in my book. *Nothing exists except atoms and empty space. All the rest is opinion.* This is not just a frivolous quote; it touches the essence of what I want to say in this chapter. The word 'atom', coined by Democritus of Abdera, comes from *atomon*, indivisible. The word 'individual' has a similar origin but in Latin: Marcus Tullius Cicero used the word *individuus*, indivisible. Individuals, it could be said, are the atoms of society. A State is a multitude of individuals, who live together on a fixed territory and recognize common laws and government.

In international law, the individual has long been neglected, but international criminal law has brought the individual back to centre stage. An individual will be the defendant in every single case before the ICC. It is interesting to note that, in academic literature on international criminal law, the individual holds a far from prominent position. The emphasis remains on the relations between States, the relations between international organizations and States, and the relations between tribunals and States. From a societal point of view, there is something to be said for this hesitation to define the position of the individual as *a*, let alone *the*, subject of international law. Martti Koskenniemi wrote in 1989:

> 'To conceptualize social life in terms of individuals freely entering into relations with each other in the great market-place of the world is merely a way to impose another grand-scale Western-liberal framework on a conflicting reality. The interminable discussion of whether the "true" subjects of international law are States or individuals fails to recognize the differences in our communal ties.'[1]

Yes, the individual in one State has different ties, rights, duties and maybe even morals than the individual in another State. Even within a State different individuals can have completely different communal ties. To be more precise, every individual is different. Every individual has a certain degree of autonomy. Well, of course, we are all contextual individuals,[2] political animals even, if you want to be Aristotelian about it, but international criminal law makes clear that every individual can be, and is, the bearer of responsibility. The ICC will put only individuals in the dock for committing genocide, war crimes, and crimes against humanity – not States, not even groups, but individuals. The interesting point here is that these three crimes are, par excellence, crimes that are committed within the context of States or groups. It is not one individual who starts a war, not one individual who embarks on a genocidal mission, not one individual who sets out to commit crimes against humanity – which the Rome Statute defines as being part of a 'widespread or systematic attack'.[3] But, be that as it may, it always takes one or more individuals actually to commit these crimes. A State is a fiction, an army is a fiction, a group is a fiction; individuals are as real as it gets in our world. The Rome Statute is an important step towards recognition of the individual in international law, international relations, and henceforth in making international law more 'real' law.

---

[1] M. Koskenniemi, *From Apology to Utopia: The Structure of International Legal Argument* (Helsinki, Finnish Lawyers' Publishing Co 1989) 499.

[2] N. MacCormick, *Questioning Sovereignty: Law, State, and Nation in the European Commonwealth* (Oxford, Oxford University Press 1999) 167-192.

[3] Rome Statute of the International Criminal Court (Rome Statute) Art. 7 para. 1 (adopted 17 July 1998, entered into force 1 July 2002) UN Doc. A/CONF.183/9.

When we make laws, when we erect courthouses, we must have a notion of what forms of human agency we want to forbid. There is always a component of order in legislation, as well as a moral component. International criminal laws are directed at individuals. I do not think criminal laws can be made and upheld without some set of ideas about individuals as moral agents. I do not think ideas about individuals as moral agents can be formed in abstraction from their flesh-and-blood reality. So we need to acknowledge the flesh-and-blood reality of individuals as a cornerstone of any system of criminal law and the international criminal law of the ICC as a special branch of criminal law. So who are those flesh-and-blood individuals who can end up in the dock of the ICC? And what is the order within which the ICC will function as the adjudicative arena? The Court has jurisdiction over certain crimes committed by certain individuals in certain, jurisdictionally relevant settings. Article 12, paragraph 2, of the Rome Statute formulates ICC jurisdiction over crimes based on the acceptance (by 'Party-ship' or declaration) of either:

> '(a) The State on the territory of which the conduct in question occurred or, if the crime was committed on board a vessel or aircraft, the State of registration of that vessel or aircraft;
> (b) The State of which the person accused of the crime is a national.'[4]

It follows from Article 12 that the ICC does not claim universal jurisdiction; it does matter for the ICC where the individual commits his crime or what nationality he has. 'Territory' and 'nationality', again two fictions. Both of these fictions are closely related to one of the most pervasive fictions of international law: sovereignty (the word derived from the Latin contraction *superanus*, in the highest position). In the next section I explore the relationship between the individual and the concept of sovereignty.

4.   SOVEREIGNTY

Sovereignty has no substance. Sovereignty as a concept has no determined meaning. The notion of a *sovereign* in the sense of Hobbes or even Austin

---

[4]   Ibid. Art. 12 para. 2.

has become an anachronism. Yet the notion of sovereignty seems to be one of the most important elements of political-legal debate. In international law the notion of sovereignty is usually connected with States. A division is often made between *internal* and *external* sovereignty, *territorial* and *legal* sovereignty. In this article I do not go into all the theories of sovereignty, the debates about watered-down sovereignty, interdependence, supra-nationality. The aim of this article is, as stated in the introduction, to explore the conceptual relationship between the individual and sovereignty in light of the complementarity principle of the ICC. My first question is whether there is a relationship between the individual and sovereignty.

To answer that question I must first define 'individual' and 'sovereignty'. In the previous paragraph I ventured to explain the concept of an individual: basically 'every human being with a pulse'. Sovereignty in my view is *power* in connection with *acceptance*, nothing more and certainly nothing less. *Power* has always been an instrumental yet polyvalent word in national and international relations and law, especially in connection with that ultimately polyvalent word *rule*.[5] Power, for this article, will be defined as the *possibility to exercise my will*. Like any definition, this one is of course fraught with philosophical difficulties, but luckily the days of Heidegger and Derrida are gone. Let me just briefly say a few things about this definition. Of course, by power I do not mean omnipotence. The concept of omnipotence is nothing but an absurd thought experiment; all and everyone's power is limited. The phrase *to exercise my will* bears not only upon my own actions, but also upon the possibility of making and changing rules for actions, be it my own or those of other individuals, and of making sure these rules are obeyed. But sovereignty, in my view, is not just raw power. That would suffice for a community of one person, but, as soon as a community is larger than that, the notion of power has to be connected with *acceptance* to amount to sov-

---

[5] See, e.g., B. Russell, *Power: A New Social Analysis*, 3rd edn. (London, George Allen & Unwin Ltd 1938); C. Schmitt, *Der Begriff des Politischen* (Berlin, Duncker & Humblodt 1963) 28-37; and the classic H.L.A. Hart, *The Concept of Law*, 2nd edn. (Oxford, Oxford University Press 1958, 1994). For a present day view on sovereignty (and Schmitt), see G. Agamben, *Homo Sacer: Sovereign Power and Bare Life* (Stanford Calif., Stanford University Press 1998). For a stimulating, yet 'Huntingtonian', view on the relationship between revolutions in ideas and revolutions in sovereignty, see D. Philpott, *Revolutions in Sovereignty: How Ideas Shaped Modern International Relations* (Princeton NJ, Princeton University Press 2001) 46-72.

ereignty. Acceptance, for this article, is the *acknowledgment of power, by free will or necessity*. If I agree to an action of another individual and do not interfere with his action, then I accept his power in that regard. If I agree to a rule that has been made by someone other than myself and do not act contrary to that rule, than I accept her power. If I do not agree by my own free will to an action by someone else or a rule made by someone else but realize that trying to prohibit or change or disobey the action or rule would cost me too much, I will see the necessity of my acceptance of her power. In the acceptance of power lies the essence of sovereignty.

The relationship between an individual and the concept of sovereignty lies in the power of that individual and/or his acceptance of power of one or more other individual(s). Because of the complexity of human interactions and coexistence, sovereignty amounts to a fictional web of power relations. All seven billion individuals on this earth accept one or more forms of power structures. The ICC has a judicial role in that intricate web we call the world. Representatives of individuals from all over the world will judge the individual sitting in the dock. To be a criminal court for the world, it has to have a well-defined legal position within the world community. To succeed, the ICC will have to prove it is a valid institution of international criminal law in the world order.

5.   WORLD ORDER

As a kid, I used to listen to old blues records of Mississippi Delta artists. They always sang about 'peoples peoples', and I would think, 'Boy, that's wrong; they can't even speak good English: People is already plural.' Now, since I have been studying international relations, the word 'peoples' has become a very familiar one. And I still think, 'Boy, that's wrong'.

Montesquieu would turn in his grave if he saw the way the ICC is positioned in a world community that is not a legal union. And maybe even that word 'community' is an overstatement of the ties that bind the seven billion individuals on this earth. For what is a community? In doctrinal language, the notion of 'in' and 'out' is instrumental to the concept and the conception of community. If there is no exclusion, there is no community. If there is no closed outer line, there is no (perfect) circle. This circle is a line of defense against unwanted influences and influxes. But that is just the external notion of community. Is that a useful idea when we talk about the world? Until the present day there has been – to my knowledge – no contact with any life form outside the world as we know it. So if we want to decide if we can call the world a community, we have to analyse the internal characteristics of a community as a demarcation of a homogenous zone of values and usages, of rights and wrongs, of common identity. In this ever more interdependent world, the existing circles are under constant pressure to change and to open up. The peoples, multitudes, individuals of the world have in the last century been in constant negotiations regarding these changes. But recent political and military developments show that the exclusionary character of existing communities, combined with a sense of normative identity and even superiority, still stands in the way of the idea of one global community. If there is a *Weltgeist* somewhere on our horizon, than the contours of its materialization are, as yet, very vague.

This – political – world is a *pluriversum*, not a *universum*.[6] Humanity, in spirit and in the flesh, may live together but not as one. There are ties, there are contracts, but I doubt if there are rules and principles that are valid for all of us individuals. I doubt if there is order in this world. Humanity can dine most pleasantly in Kant's charming bistro *Zum ewigen Frieden* [Perpetual Peace], but 'round midnight, in the dark woods, humanity turns into a Hobbesian *lupus*. If there is such a thing as *world order*, then it is built on foundations of violence.[7] Recognition of sovereignty, treaties of international law, borders, flags and the Olympic Games: These are all mere rituals that sanctify the *status quo*. Or are they? Maybe we are wiser than our forefathers, and maybe we realize that the alternative to our feeble concept of *world order* is ubiquitous violence. Maybe the delegation of part of our individual autonomy to our 'home' State in pursuit of a Kantian notion of a league of nations, with a form of *Contrat Social* between States, is not such a bad concept.[8] Maybe.

Enough with theoretical vagaries, time for the law. The name of Montesquieu is already mentioned. Now let's see, is there a *trias politica* in the

---

[6] Schmitt (n. 5) 54.

[7] H. Bull, *The Anarchical Society: A Study of Order in World Politics* (New York, Columbia University Press 1977) 88.

[8] I. Kant, *The Metaphysics of Morals* (Cambridge, Cambridge University Press 1996) 115.

world? No. There is no legislative branch. There is no executive branch. But, for the gravest of crimes, there is a court: the ICC. Would such a situation be acceptable in a State? Probably not. Is that a problem? Difficult question. The answer depends largely on the demands you set and the vision you formulate of international criminal law.

6. INTERNATIONAL CRIMINAL LAW

In 1927, in the *Lotus* case, a dispute between Turkey and France about criminal jurisdiction over acts committed on the high seas, the Permanent Court of International Justice (PCIJ) gave its now classic definition of international law:

> 'International law governs relations between independent states. The rule of law binding upon states therefore emanates from their own free will as expressed in conventions or usages generally accepted as expressing principles of law and in order to regulate the relations between these co-existing independent communities or with a view to the achievement of common aims.'[9]

The Law of Nations is a law between, not above, sovereign States.[10] Over the last century, this has, by and large, been the leading view among scholars of international law. The rule of law 'emanates from' the 'own free will' of sovereign States – it is almost as if the PCIJ itself regards States as anthropomorphous; they have 'their own free will'. This may be the right language: What more is a State than the sum of all the individuals that live on its territory?

International criminal law, it was said in the previous section, is a special branch of criminal law; but it is also closely connected to the concept of international law. What does this say about the nature of international criminal law? Although it is generally accepted that international law has arrived

---

[9] *Case of the S.S. 'Lotus' (France v. Turkey)*, *PCIJ Rep Series A* No. 10 (1927) 18.

[10] L. Oppenheim, *International Law: A Treatise, Vol. I Peace*, 8th edn. (D. McKay, New York 1955) 20. See also, D. Held, 'Law of States, Law of Peoples: Three Models of Sovereignty', 8 *Legal Theory* (2002) 1.

in a post-ontological era,[11] the exact nature of its existence is far from clear. Where does the legitimacy of an international criminal tribunal come from? What are the requirements for its success, in legal and political terms? How can we make sure that we never have to 'play courthouse' again, as in Nuremberg and especially Tokyo, 'the worst hypocrisy in recorded history',[12] or have to be 'creative' with jurisdiction, like in the *Eichmann* case? Since the days of Kant, international law draws its legitimacy from rationalist arguments about interdependence and harmony of interests: We are all in this together.[13] But in two cases that seem very relevant for the development of international criminal law, *Pinochet*[14] and *Yerodia*,[15] different views of international law were expressed, as Philippe Sands observes:

'The judgment of the House of Lords (a national court) in *Pinochet* and of the ICJ [International Court of Justice] in *Yerodia* reflect, in my opinion, a struggle between two competing visions of international law. For the majority in the House of Lords, international law is treated as a set of rules the primary purpose of which is to give effect to a set of broadly shared values, including a commitment to rooting out impunity for the gravest international crimes. The other vision, that reflected in the judgment of the ICJ, sees the rules of international law as being intended principally to facilitate relations between states, which remain the principal international actors.'[16]

---

[11] T.M. Franck, *Fairness in International Law and Institutions* (Oxford, Oxford University Press 1995) 6. On the question 'Is international law really law?', see H.L.A. Hart, *The Concept of Law*, 2nd edn. (Oxford, Oxord University Press 1994) 213-237.

[12] B.V.A. Röling and A. Cassese, *The Tokyo Trial and Beyond* (Cambridge, Polity Press 1993) 112. These words were spoken by General Willoughby, head of G2 in Japan, to Röling privately, and Röling does not seem to disagree.

[13] M. Koskenniemi and P. Leino, 'Fragmentation of International Law? Postmodern Anxieties', 15 *Leiden J Intl L* (2002), 553, 556.

[14] *R v. Bow Street Metropolitan Stipendiary Magistrate and others, ex parte Pinochet Ugarte*, [2000] 1 AC 147 (HL).

[15] *Case Concerning the Arrest Warrant of 11 April 2000 (Democratic Republic of the Congo v. Belgium)*, [2002] *ICJ Rep.* 1. See, in particular, the impressive joint separate opinion of Judges Higgins, Kooijmans and Buergenthal and the brilliantly courageous dissenting opinion by Judge Van den Wyngaert.

[16] P. Sands, 'After Pinochet: The Role of International Courts', in P. Sands (ed.), *From Nuremberg to The Hague: The Future of International Criminal Justice* (Cambridge, Cambridge University Press 2003) 103.

The tension between these two competing visions could be of the utmost importance for the success of the ICC, especially in light of the complementarity principle. The court will rely heavily on the cooperation of States, for it is supranational by name, but not by 'physical' power. Where exactly does this supranational body stand in a world where supranationality is not a matter of community but of *pacta*? States are seen by some as a *species of superman*.[17] I would call the ICC a *species of supraman*. And I am sceptical about the powers of this *supraman* against strong opposition. More than half of the world's population is not represented in the Assembly of States Parties to the ICC, so its work will stand in continuous tension with the ever changing world community. The judicial words of the Court will hardly be backed up by swords. So, for the sake of the success of the ICC, we must hope that the *Pinochet* vision will eventually prevail over the *Yerodia* vision. In order to make sure that States assist and support the ICC as much as possible and thus help the ICC 'give effect to a set of broadly shared values, including a commitment to rooting out impunity for the gravest international crimes',[18] there is a rather strong emphasis on the diplomacy of the ICC: Both the President and the Prosecutor work very hard to promote their Court. In order to secure future cooperation regarding complementarity, collecting evidence, arrest, investigation, et cetera, knowledge of the corridors of diplomacy could prove very important for the Court. But we should be careful:

> 'When criminal law and diplomacy meet the result is likely to be either undermining diplomatic freedom of action – or turning criminal justice into show trials. Any middle ground here is both narrow and slippery.'[19]

Rather implicit, but no less important, in the clash between the two competing visions of *Pinochet* and *Yerodia* is the difference in approach regarding the position of the individual. The ICJ, of course, is by its nature a court where States are the principal actors but that does not necessarily imply that there is no regard for the interest of individuals. In *Yerodia* the ICJ majority opinion expresses a vision of rules of international law as being intended

---

[17] Hart (n. 11) 221.
[18] Sands (n. 16).
[19] Koskenniemi and Leino (n. 13) 578.

principally to facilitate relations between States, which remain the principal international actors. If that would be the prevailing vision in the world, then international criminal law can hardly be expected to deviate too far from that vision. This would mean that, with respect to the accused in an investigation, prosecution or trial, States could be expected to act in accordance with the aforementioned vision. This will not always be in favor of the operation of the ICC, and it will have all kinds of possible effects on the position of the individual. From the accused standpoint, this can turn out either positively or negatively: He can walk because of obstruction by the State in which he is living; he can become a sacrificial lamb; his rights can be trampled; he can be let off the hook for lack of evidence resulting from the lack of State cooperation. But the importance of this all is that many of the relevant decisions will be based on issues that go 'over his head', and it is highly questionable if that could account for a sound system of criminal law. Regarding complementarity, there will always be tension between the claims concerning the willingness and ability to prosecute of a State that would normally have jurisdiction over a case and the vision of the Prosecutor and/or the Court. The *Yerodia* attitude towards supranational harmony would not help the ICC in that regard.

The *Pinochet* vision seems to lean more towards respect for the individual, which means more respect not only for the rights of an individual but also for his responsibilities. The notion of 'broadly shared values'[20] is by its nature a notion of people, groups, and individuals, and it does not require the concept of a State to be upheld. If the ICC can come to be a *champion* of those 'broadly shared values',[21] then, in the *Pinochet* vision, it could become an important factor in the promulgation of international justice. Not that the success of the ICC is not a valuable cause in itself, but the underlying values that would be promoted by the Court make its success a cause for which it is worth striving. It is striking that *Pinochet* was decided by a national court. If all national courts would adopt a similar vision as that expressed by Browne-Wilkinson and his fellow judges, than the complementarity principle of the ICC would certainly have its effect – or not need to have any effect anymore.

---

[20] Sands (n. 16).
[21] Ibid.

7. COMPLEMENTARITY

In this section I focus on the issue of admissibility under Article 17 of the Rome Statute,[22] where the accused claims that a State that is not party to the Rome Statute has jurisdiction over his case and will exercise or has exercised that jurisdiction genuinely in the sense of Article 17. I use the fictitious *Doran* case as an example to explore the relationship between the individual and the concept of sovereignty in light of the complementarity principle of the ICC. To be a bit more specific, I explore *judicial sovereignty*, by which I mean the right and power to adjudicate. For now I will focus on the individual in a criminal case: Who can judge me?

---

[22] Art. 17 of the Rome Statute (n. 3) provides:

'Article 17

Issues of admissibility

1. Having regard to paragraph 10 of the Preamble and article 1, the Court shall determine that a case is inadmissible where:

(a) The case is being investigated or prosecuted by a State which has jurisdiction over it, unless the State is unwilling or unable genuinely to carry out the investigation or prosecution;

(b) The case has been investigated by a State which has jurisdiction over it and the State has decided not to prosecute the person concerned, unless the decision resulted from the unwillingness or inability of the State genuinely to prosecute;

(c) The person concerned has already been tried for conduct which is the subject of the complaint, and a trial by the Court is not permitted under article 20, paragraph 3;

(d) The case is not of sufficient gravity to justify further action by the Court.

2. In order to determine unwillingness in a particular case, the Court shall consider, having regard to the principles of due process recognized by international law, whether one or more of the following exist, as applicable:

(a) The proceedings were or are being undertaken or the national decision was made for the purpose of shielding the person concerned from criminal responsibility for crimes within the jurisdiction of the Court referred to in article 5;

(b) There has been an unjustified delay in the proceedings which in the circumstances is inconsistent with an intent to bring the person concerned to justice;

(c) The proceedings were not or are not being conducted independently or impartially, and they were or are being conducted in a manner which, in the circumstances, is inconsistent with an intent to bring the person concerned to justice.

3. In order to determine inability in a particular case, the Court shall consider whether, due to a total or substantial collapse or unavailability of its national judicial system, the State is unable to obtain the accused or the necessary evidence and testimony or otherwise unable to carry out its proceedings.'

'A people judges itself through those of its fellow citizens whom it des-ignates as its representatives for this by a free choice …'.[23] This may be a 'Western-liberal'[24] view of adjudication, but let's run with it for a while. Who are my fellow citizens? Who are the 18 judges of the ICC?[25] What is my relation to those people? And is this relevant? It is a widely accepted principle of law that people will be judged by people with whom they share some form of community or by people of a community with whom they have had interaction relevant to the legal issue for which they are brought to justice. In continental European law there is the principle of *jus de non evocando*, the rule that nobody can, against his will, be removed from the judge that is established by law. This point was raised by the defense in the *Tadić* case, but the International Criminal Tribunal for the former Yugosla-via (ICTY) dismissed it on the grounds that this rule only applied to the creation of politically motivated, special tribunals and that the ICTY was certainly not such a tribunal. To quote the ICTY Appeals Chamber:

'[O]ne cannot but rejoice at the thought that universal jurisdiction being nowadays acknowledged in the case of international crimes, a person sus-pected of such offences may finally be brought before an international judi-cial body for a dispassionate consideration of his indictment by impartial, independent and disinterested judges coming, as it happens here, from all continents of the world.'[26]

Now, whatever we may think of this interesting display of self love, it is rather beside the point. The question is whether an individual can be re-moved from his *juge naturel*. This of course depends on how you define this *juge naturel*. I think it would be safe to say that the judges of the ICTY

---

[23] Kant (n. 8) 94.

[24] Koskenniemi (n. 1).

[25] Art. 36, para. 8a, of the Rome Statute (n. 3) provides:
The States Parties shall, in the selection of judges, take into account the need, within the membership of the Court, for:
(i)   The representation of the principal legal systems of the world;
(ii)   Equitable geographical representation; and
(iii) A fair representation of female and male judges.

[26] *Prosecutor* v. *Tadić* (Decision on the Defence Motion for Interlocutory Appeal on Jurisdiction) ICTY-94-1-AR72 para. 62 (2 October 1995) 35 *ILM* (1996), 32, 53.

were not *juges naturels* for Dusan Tadić. And I think it would be less safe, but very defendable, to state that the judges of the ICC *can* be seen as *juges naturels* at least for individuals who are nationals of States Parties to the Rome Statute.

The Trial Chamber in that same *Tadić* case raised another question, which is important for my argument, namely that 'it is by no means clear that an individual has standing to raise this point.'[27] This statement opens an immensely wide range of questions, legal, historical and philosophical, about the position and the rights of an individual in a criminal procedure, as well as about the relationship between an individual and a State with regard to the jurisdiction of a court.[28] Before I embarked on an investigative journey here, I deemed it wise to look at the legal actuality before us, Article 19, paragraph 2, of the Rome Statute states:

'Article 19(2)
Challenges to the admissibility of a case on the grounds referred to in article 17 or challenges to the jurisdiction of the Court may be made by:
(a) An accused or a person for whom a warrant of arrest or a summons to appear has been issued under article 58;
(b) A State which has jurisdiction over a case, on the ground that it is investigating or prosecuting the case or has investigated or prosecuted; or
(c) A State from which acceptance of jurisdiction is required under article 12.'[29]

So the delegates at the Rome Conference thought about this point and decided that an individual can challenge the jurisdiction of the Court and the admissibility of his case, based on the principle of complementarity as laid down in Article 17 of the Statute. Of course there is no mention of a *juge naturel* in Article 17, but it does give preference to the national court that would normally have jurisdiction. The individual does have standing in this matter before the ICC. The individual can call upon the judicial sovereignty

---

[27] *Prosecutor* v. *Tadić* (Decision on the Defence Motion on Jurisdiction) ICTY-94-1-T para. 37 (10 August 1995).

[28] This will actually be a central question in the historical research that I will do for my Ph.D. dissertation, partly at the Max Planck Institute for European Legal History in Frankfurt.

[29] Rome Statute (n. 3) Art. 19 para. 2.

of a State. But what good will this do for the individual? His case can still be qualified as admissible by the Prosecutor or the Pre-Trial Chamber if they consider the relevant State to be unable or unwilling genuinely to carry out a judicial procedure concerning this individual. What is the role of the State here? And what are the possibilities for the defendant?

Sovereignty consists of power and acceptance. Judicial sovereignty, a qualified version of sovereignty, is the power to adjudicate and the acceptance of that power. This power rests usually with the judicial branch in a State. As a general rule, the judiciary is embedded in a power structure which vaguely resembles the antique concept of *trias politica*. If an individual commits a crime in his own country, he will – ideally – be brought before a judge in his own country. This judge will render a verdict and the individual will have to obey that verdict. If an individual commits a crime in a country other than his own, he will – again ideally – be brought before a judge in that country or a judge in his own country. Under the complementarity principle, an individual may challenge the admissibility of his case on the basis of the fact that a State will exercise its jurisdiction. The ICC, represented by the Prosecutor or one of the chambers, will assess whether the national procedure to which the defendant refers is on par with the ICC standard. The case could still be admissible when the State is unable or unwilling genuinely to carry out these procedures or when a past procedure can be qualified as reflecting this same inability or unwillingness. So the ICC will judge the procedure in the national State. Is this an infringement on the State's sovereignty? Before we answer that question, let's look at what really will happen in a case like this. How will the ICC go about its work when an individual has brought forward a challenge to admissibility?

'Rule 58

Proceedings under article 19

1. A request or application made under article 19 shall be in writing and contain the basis for it.

2. When a Chamber receives a request or application raising a challenge or question concerning its jurisdiction or the admissibility of a case in accordance with article 19, paragraph 2 or 3, or is acting on its own motion as provided for in article 19, paragraph 1, it shall decide on the procedure to be followed and may take appropriate measures for the proper conduct of the proceedings. It may hold a hearing. It may join the challenge or question to a

confirmation or a trial proceeding as long as this does not cause undue delay, and in this circumstance shall hear and decide on the challenge or question first.

3. The Court shall transmit a request or application received under sub-rule 2 to the Prosecutor and to the person referred to in article 19, paragraph 2, who has been surrendered to the Court or who has appeared voluntarily or pursuant to a summons, and shall allow them to submit written observations to the request or application within a period of time determined by the Chamber.

4. The Court shall rule on any challenge or question of jurisdiction first and then on any challenge or question of admissibility.'[30]

There is a lot of discretionary power for the Chamber here. Reading this article, I cannot see how exactly the Chamber will act upon a request under Article 19, paragraph 2(a). Will it ask the accused to deliver the relevant information regarding his challenge? Will the accused be asked to contact the State on this matter? Or will the Chamber contact the State itself? Or will it ask the Prosecutor to contact the State? Or will there be some indirect manner in which this matter will be investigated? Where exactly lies the burden of proof? Does the individual have to prove his claim that there are or have been sufficient criminal proceedings against him in his own country? What if the State refuses to cooperate on the basis that it does not recognize the powers of the ICC? Will there be any question of the benefit of the doubt for the defendant? And if there is a hearing or trial proceeding, will it be seen as part of 'the trial' of the accused, for instance in the sense of Article 63 of the Rome Statute, which requires that the trial take place in the presence of the accused? And if the State demands, not for reasons of national security, but for reasons of the integrity of the national criminal proceeding against the accused, that the accused cannot be present during the hearing or trial proceeding or that there cannot be disclosure of relevant papers, what will the rights of the defendant be? And what about Article 90 of the Rome Statute? Does that not provide for a rather awkward triangular relationship between a non-State Party, a State Party and the ICC, regarding the requirements and priority rules of transfer/extradition? A lot of questions, some of them easy to answer, some of them maybe a bit harder, but finding those answers is not the objective of this article. I am interested in

---

[30] Rules of Procedure and Evidence ICC-ASP/1/3 (September 2002) Rule 58.

the bearing these issues have on the question of sovereignty with regard to the non-party State and the individual.

I would argue – and this a view that is broadly shared I think – that complementarity does have an effect on the sovereignty of a State, in the sense of *power* and *acceptance*. First, the principle of complementarity is already a *procedural* infringement on the relationship between an individual and a State. The individual has to address the ICC with his claim, as we see in Rule 58. That is already a first step in the 'sovereignty chain'. And then, if the ICC deems any form of cooperation by the State necessary to establish the lack of inability or unwillingness, then this is also an intrusion into the State's sovereignty, if non-cooperation in this case would mean that the ICC concludes that there are not enough grounds to transfer the accused to that State. And if there are or have been criminal proceedings regarding the accused and the State gives the ICC a report of them, and the ICC would, for instance, judge that these proceedings were held for the purpose of shielding the accused, then of course this has some bearing on the State's sovereignty, when it means that the accused would stay in the custody and powers of the ICC, a fact which is not accepted by the State, but with regard to which it has not the powers to take any action. And if that State would take action against the ICC, for instance by liberating the accused and bringing him home to their country, then that act would certainly touch on aspects of sovereignty.

Back to Doran now, our fictitious individual. Where do the issues of sovereignty lie for him?

8.   THE *DORAN* CASE

Doran is sitting in his cell, contemplating what to do. First he decides to challenge the jurisdiction of the ICC. At the time of the alleged commission of the alleged crime, he was a national of Overland, which was not a State Party. Some of the alleged crimes were allegedly committed on the territory of Overland, which was not a State Party. So there is no basis in Article 12 for jurisdiction, he claims. That same territory is now the territory of Majorland, which is a State Party, but that does not suffice to give the ICC jurisdiction, Doran claims. Now, whatever the ruling of the ICC may be on this point, there is certainly a sovereignty issue at hand here. State sover-

eignty cannot exist without some notion of the individuals who are constitutive elements of that State. Doran was a national of Overland. He accepted the power of Overland. Overland had sovereignty with regards to
him. Now Doran is a national of Minorland. He accepts the power of
Minorland. Minorland has sovereignty with regards to him. But neither
Overland nor Minorland accepted the powers of the ICC. Still the ICC claims
jurisdiction on the basis of its relationship with Majorland. What does this
mean for the notion of sovereignty for this individual? I will not answer this
question because there are too many hypotheses in this story, but these are
questions that could be asked within a few years.

Making further use of Article 17, Doran then challenges the admissibility of his case. He says the authorities of Minorland will investigate and
prosecute his case. He decides to challenge the admissibility of his case on
the basis of Article 19, paragraph 2(a), of the Rome Statute. He writes a
brief to that effect and makes sure the Registrar gets it. The Prosecutor of
the ICC, as well as the Pre-Trial Chamber, rejects this claim, if only because the judicial apparatus in Minorland is in a very nascent state. And the
judiciary, as well as the government, is manned with friends of Doran, who
will, in the view of the ICC, shield him from genuine prosecution. The ICC
has decided all of this, without hearing or seeking direct contact with
Minorland, but based on reports of international organizations. But then
Minorland brings a challenge of its own, based on the same complementarity
issue. This time the ICC can be very swift with its decision: It is the same
decision as that on the personal request of Doran. Then Minorland requests
extradition from Majorland, but without any success; after consulting with
the ICC, Majorland decides to transfer Doran to The Hague. So whatever
Doran claims, whatever Minorland claims, for the next few years, this man
will have the detention unit in Scheveningen as his postal address.

What does this mean for the relationship among Doran, the concept of
sovereignty and the ICC in its complementary nature? Doran has to answer
to the ICC, so there is a relationship of judicial sovereignty between him
and the ICC *via* Majorland – or maybe even in a more direct sense? Is the
ICC a court for all the individuals of the world, and are we therefore all
'world citizens'? It seems to me that the answer to that question could lie
somewhere in the house of mirrors that is the complementarity principle.

9. CONCLUSION

In this short chapter I have tried to raise some questions regarding the relationship between the individual and the concept of sovereignty in light of the complementarity principle of the ICC. An individual has a relationship with the State in which he lives. States have relations with each other. States have relations with supranational institutions. The ICC as a supranational institution has relations with States. The ICC as a supranational institution has relations with individuals, the accused. The communication between the ICC and an individual is a direct one, not through the lines or ranks of States. The complementarity principle at first glance bears on the relations between the ICC and States, whether party to the Rome Statute or not, but the ultimate subject in a complementarity question is the individual. For an individual can be faced with judicial powers that he never saw as part of his own concept of sovereignty. The ICC as the 'world criminal court' is a – hesitant – step towards the conceptualization of individuals as 'world citizens'.

COMMENTS ON CHAPTERS 1 AND 2 OF FRÉDÉRIC MÉGRET AND GERBEN KOR

*Bardo Fassbender**

Complementarity, as it has been very ably discussed in the two chapters by Frédéric Mégret and Gerben Kor, is a new principle in the international legal order. Right now its field of application is a very limited one, but there is a chance of its being transferred to other areas of international law beyond international criminal law and the jurisdiction of the ICC. Therefore, it could be interesting to see whether and, if so, how this new principle of complementarity is related to other, older principles of international or supranational law.

One principle, or concept, which comes to mind in this context is that of subsidiarity. There seems to be a similarity, in that both principles, complementarity and subsidiarity, give priority to the lower level in of a hierarchy in a system of public functions. Even if the notion of subsidiarity has entered the sphere of public law only in recent times, subsidiarity is, in substance, a classical concept of the constitutional law of federal States, for instance Germany or Switzerland. In the present German Constitution, the 'Basic Law' [Grundgesetz], Article 30, which deals with the general division of authority between the Federation and the individual German states [*Länder*], provides: 'Except as otherwise provided or permitted by this Basic Law, the exercise of state powers and the discharge of state functions is a matter for the *Länder*.'

It is well-known that subsidiarity has also been integrated into the law of the European Union.[1] This principle was confirmed in the recently signed

---

* Associate Professor, Faculty of Law, Humboldt University Berlin.

[1] The EC Treaty (Treaty of Rome, as amended), Art. 5, as presently in force, provides: (1) The Community shall act within the limits of the powers conferred upon it by this Treaty and of the objectives assigned to it therein.

J.K. Kleffner & G. Kor (eds.), Complementary Views on Complementarity
© 2006, T·M·C·ASSER PRESS, *The Hague, The Netherlands and the Authors*

Treaty Establishing a Constitution for Europe, in which it was combined with the technical principle of conferral.[2] According to Article I-11, paragraph 3:

> 'Under the principle of subsidiarity, in areas which do not fall within its exclusive competence, the Union shall act only if and insofar as the objectives of the proposed action cannot be sufficiently achieved by the Member States, either at central level or at regional and local level, but can rather, by reason of the scale or effects of the proposed action, be better achieved at Union level.'[3]

So far, subsidiarity is not a principle of (general) international law, but it is nonetheless possible that, in the not so distant future, especially in the process of a further expansion of powers of international organizations and institutions, it will become one. It could evolve into a rule of the constitutional law of the international community,[4] governing the general distribution of competences between the organs of that community on the one hand, and the individual Member States of the international community on the other, and complementing the principle of sovereign equality.

The two chapters reflect quite different general attitudes of their authors. Frédéric's chapter, asking the crucial question 'Why would States want to join the ICC?', is written in a mood of friendly realism. I think it reflects a

---

(2) In areas which do not fall within its exclusive competence, the Community shall take action, in accordance with the principle of subsidiarity, only if and in so far as the objectives of the proposed action cannot be sufficiently achieved by the Member States and can therefore, by reason of the scale or effects of the proposed action, be better achieved by the Community.
(3) Any action by the Community shall not go beyond what is necessary to achieve the objectives of this Treaty.

[2] See Treaty Establishing a Constitution for Europe, Art. I-11.

[3] Ibid. Art. I-11 para. 3. See, also, the Protocol 2 on the Application of the Principles of Subsidiarity and Proportionality annexed to the Treaty Establishing a Constitution for Europe.

[4] For the meaning of the term 'international community', see B. Fassbender, 'The United Nations Charter as Constitution of the International Community', 36 *Columbia J Transnational L* (1998), 529-619; B. Fassbender, 'The Meaning of International Constitutional Law', in R. MacDonald and D.M. Johnston (eds.), *Towards World Constitutionalism: Issues in the Legal Ordering of the World Community* (The Hague, Martinus Nijhoff 2005 forthcoming).

French education in thinking in terms of national interest. In comparison, Gerben's chapter is an example of what one could call philosophical fundamentalism, coming up with a really impressive row of fundamental questions and challenging a number of conventional definitions. Astonishingly, both chapters have a rather optimistic ending: Frédéric concludes by saying that 'sovereignty is much less untrammelled and absolute power, as a considerable power that is nonetheless thoroughly constrained by international law'[5] and, in a phrase echoing the writings of Philip Allott, that the ICC is 'part of the international community's own process of constitutionalization and self-realization.'[6] I very much agree with this view. Gerben writes: 'The ICC as the 'world criminal court' is a – hesitant – step towards the conceptualization of individuals as 'world citizens'.'[7] This is a beautiful vision of the future, I think. It reminds me of a similar remark by Judge Sir Hersch Lauterpacht of the 1950s in which he said that the judges of the International Court of Justice should act as citizens of the universal *civitas maxima*.

In the chapter written by Frédéric Mégret, three basic assumptions are made. The first is that States make rational choices. The second is that States are actors. And the third is that States act according to what they see as their national interest. That is a lot, these three taken together. There is a paradox – the question whether we can rationally analyse irrationality. So maybe we have no choice but to assume that States make rational choices. However, I am not so sure about that. One important aspect (only one of several) we would have to consider in order to assess the reasons why governments ratify the ICC Statute is the aspect of 'political psychology', or 'the psychology of international relations'. To be sure, Frédéric did consider some of this in his chapter. At times, there are certain general trends in the international system, a generally shared feeling that a train is riding in a certain direction and that it is a good thing to jump on at this moment. And in the end it is politicians who make these decisions, rather than the officials in the foreign ministries. Maybe the politicians do not think as much as Frédéric did in his chapter but 'just do it'. On the other hand, you can, of course, point to a number of countries which have not taken this decision to join the

---

[5] F. Mégret 51.
[6] Ibid.
[7] G. Kor 71.

ICC, and they must have thought about it, arriving at this negative result.

Then on to sovereignty and international law. Frédéric asked whether sovereignty can be understood as a power of States defined by international law. I very much agree with this perspective.[8] I personally understand sovereignty of States as a right of States to a 'space of autonomy', as defined by international law or, to be more precise, by the constitutional rules of international law. It is not an absolute power in the old sense but a legally defined and restrained power of a State as an actor in international law. Does the acceptance of the jurisdiction of the ICC, pursuant to Article 12 of the Rome Statute, as modified by the principle of complementarity under Article 17, constitute a limitation on sovereignty? Following a conventional view, one would answer this question in the negative and say that the respective obligation has been freely accepted by a State by way of treaty-making. States which have ratified the Rome Statute have accepted the Court's jurisdiction in the exercise of their sovereign powers. For the time being, it is inconceivable that the respective treaty rules become part of general international law, in which case one would have to interpret them as yet another step on a long road of limitations on the 'old sovereignty' of the 19th and early 20th century.

Gerben Kor's chapter about complementarity and national sovereignty asks, as I said before, a row of fundamental questions and offers an impressive critique of conventional definitions. The speaker tries to make us think again about the concepts of sovereignty and community and about the role of the individual in international law. I very much like this approach of going back to the roots. In an ever more complex and refined field, it is indispensable from time to time to pause for a moment and re-evaluate the basic notions upon which our modern intricate conceptions are built. I like the title Gerben has chosen for his contribution: 'Sovereignty in the Dock'. Indeed, sovereignty has been held responsible for many defects of international law and the international order in general. Varying this title, and thinking of sovereignty as an old steamer in a harbour, one could also say, 'sovereignty in the docks', and wonder whether some day it will again sail away on the open sea to faraway shores.

---

[8]   B. Fassbender, 'Sovereignty and Constitutionalism in International Law', in N. Walker (ed.), *Sovereignty in Transition* (Oxford, Hart Publishing 2003) 115-143.

Gerben defines sovereignty as a power (of someone) being accepted (by somebody else) 'by free will or necessity'.[9] I was reminded of an old German concept, *Herrschaft*, which seems to express just this. Describing two competing views of international law, and following Professor Philippe Sands, Gerben refers, on the one hand, to the *Pinochet* judgment of the House of Lords,[10] and, on the other hand, to the *Arrest Warrant* judgment of the International Court of Justice.[11] The first vision sees international law as a set of broadly shared values. The second sees international law as (only) facilitating relations between States, which, in my view, is really an outdated idea. Using again a German term, it understands international law as a *Verkehrsrecht*, or law of communications and transport, a technical means of facilitating the exchange of goods and transborder contacts of people. I think we cannot possibly go back to this 19th century concept of international law; doing so would mean to ignore the paradigmatic change which was brought about by the United Nations Charter in 1945. 'The *Pinochet* vision', Gerben concludes, 'seems to lean more towards respect for the individual, which means more respect not only for the rights of an individual but also for his responsibilities.'[12] This emphasis on the individual is perhaps the most characteristic trait of the UN Charter. Of course we know that all that was achieved in the past needs to be revitalized and achieved again. It is not so that the victory in human progress of 1945 is there once and for all, but it is our task to give new life to it, time and again. And perhaps the ICC will indeed become a champion of international law as a set of broadly shared values.

My brief remarks cannot possibly do justice to the wealth of ideas expressed in the two chapters. Everybody interested in the importance of the jurisdiction of the ICC 'beyond the realm of international criminal law', that is for the development of the general relationship between States and the organized international community, should read these chapters with her or his greatest attention.

---

[9] G. Kor 58.

[10] *R* v. *Bow Street Metropolitan Stipendiary Magistrate and others, ex parte Pinochet Ugarte*, House of Lords, [2000] 1 AC 147.

[11] *Case Concerning the Arrest Warrant of 11 April 2000 (Democratic Republic of the Congo* v. *Belgium)*, [2002] *ICJ Rep.* 1.

[12] G. Kor 63.

Chapter 3
COMPLEMENTARITY AS A CATALYST FOR COMPLIANCE

*Jann K. Kleffner**

The principle of complementarity in the Rome Statute can be conceptualized in various ways, some of which are addressed in other contributions to the roundtable. The epistomological concept of complementarity[1] suggests that these different conceptualizations are indispensable and together necessary for an exhaustive understanding of complementarity in the Rome Statute.

The present contribution focuses on one such conceptualization in particular. It takes a functional perspective and proceeds from the hypothesis that complementarity serves as a catalyst for national criminal jurisdictions

---

* Assistant Professor, Amsterdam Center for International Law, Faculty of Law, University of Amsterdam.

[1] The origin of complementarity as an epistemological concept is atomic physics. It denotes that two descriptions, though incompatible because they describe mutually exclusive observations, are both indispensable and together necessary for an exhaustive description because the conditions of observation influence the object under investigation. Such a conceptualization of complementarity is intrinsically linked to the name Niels Bohr, a Danish physicist, who initially developed the notion in response to the epistemological difficulties in understanding the nature of light. As some experiments showed light to be particles while others showed that it behaved like waves, Bohr asserted that these two descriptions, although incompatible because mutually exclusive, are 'complementary' in order to describe the nature of light exhaustively. In his words, the two descriptions 'represent equally essential knowledge about atomic systems and together exhaust this knowledge'. N. Bohr, *Atomic Physics and Human Knowledge* (New York, Wiley 1958) 74. In Bohr's view, not only practical considerations lead to such a conclusion, but also the fact that the conditions of observation, such as an experimental device, in atomic physics influence the object under investigation. The significance of Bohr's assertion was not confined to atomic physics, however, but was subsequently considered by him as a means to clarify epistemological problems in other sciences, including biology, psychology and philosophy and taken up by others in these and other fields. For an overview, see E. Rasmussen, *Complementarity and Political Science* (Odense, University Press of Southern Denmark 1987) 4-12.

J.K. Kleffner & G. Kor (eds.), Complementary Views on Complementarity
© 2006, T·M·C·Asser Press, The Hague, The Netherlands and the Authors

to investigate and prosecute the core crimes of genocide, crimes against humanity and war crimes. As such a *catalyst for compliance,* complementarity is understood as aiming to induce and facilitate the compliance of States with their obligation 'to exercise [their] criminal jurisdiction over those responsible for international crimes',[2] which underlies the Rome Statute.

The way in and extent to which complementarity can fulfil its catalyst role is determined by a variety of factors. At this early stage of the Court's functioning, it would be premature to attempt to come to any firm conclusions as to these *determinants,* however. Absent extensive practice, let alone jurisprudence on matters of admissibility, any inference drawn from the actual operationalization of complementarity by the Court cannot be anything but tentative. Such a provisional assessment may nonetheless provide a first step in the identification of determinants, which may further our understanding of the ICC's potential to fulfil its catalyst role and the challenges and limitations that the Court will face in that regard.

The hypothesis that complementarity functions as a catalyst for compliance entails the idea that determining the success or failure of the ICC includes, as one of its components to consider, complementarity's *impact on national criminal jurisdictions.* An analysis of this impact is an integral part of assessing whether the object and purpose of the Rome Statute is achieved. One question of a methodological nature that arises in connection with such an analysis is how this impact can be measured.

The present contribution addresses the aforementioned issues and is structured as follows. The first section introduces the elements of the formal framework of complementarity[3] in support of a conceptualization of

---

[2] Rome Statute of the International Criminal Court (Rome Statute) preamble para. 6 (adopted 17 July 1998, entered into force 1 July 2002) UN Doc. A/CONF.183/9.

[3] The formal framework of complementarity is understood here as the substantive aspects (Rome Statute (n. 2) Art. 17 and Art. 20 para. 3 and Rules of Procedure and Evidence (Rules) Rule 51 ICC-ASP/1/3 (September 2002)) and the procedural setting of complementarity (Rome Statute (n. 2) Arts 15, 18, 19, 53 and Rules 48, 51-62, 133). While complementarity is also related to other aspects, chief among which is Rome Statute (n. 2) Part 9, 'International Cooperation and Judicial Assistance', Arts 86-102; Rules 176-197, these aspects will in the following be discarded from our analysis. On the latter, see, e.g., ICC Office of the Prosecutor 'Informal Expert Paper: Fact-finding and Investigative Functions of the Office of the Prosecutor, including International Co-operation' (2003) paras. 22-

complementarity as a catalyst for compliance, the limitations inherent in that formal framework, as well as the further refinement of the catalyst function of complementarity by the Court, and, at this point in time, centrally within it the Office of the Prosecutor (OTP). It then turns to an identification of the determinants, which (are likely to) influence the impact of complementarity on national investigations and prosecutions, taking into account the marginal practice that is available to date. The last section is devoted to some preliminary observations on the impact on national enforcement with special attention being paid to methodological aspects of measuring this impact.

1. Complementarity's Catalyst Function

Several elements of the principle of complementarity support its being conceptualized as a catalyst for compliance. The most *general feature* of complementarity in that regard lies in the affirmation that national criminal jurisdictions bear the primary responsibility for the repression of the core crimes. Complementarity thereby creates a presumption in favour of repressive measures on the national level, which in and of itself may generate a catalyst effect. Such effect is already measurable with regard to the adoption of implementing laws that create the legislative framework for national investigations and prosecutions.[4]

---

47 <http://www.icc-cpi.int/library/organs/otp/complementarity.pdf> (21 July 2005); B. Swart and G. Sluiter, 'The International Criminal Court and International Criminal Co-operation', in H. von Hebel, J. Lammers and J. Schukking (eds.), *Reflections on the International Criminal Court: Essays in Honour of Adriaan Bos* (The Hague, T.M.C. Asser Press 1999) 91, 105-107.

[4] While the Rome Statute does not contain any express obligation for States to implement its substantive provisions, States frequently refer to the principle of complementarity as warranting implementation. Although complementarity may not be the only factor in the increased adoption of implementing legislation, these references indicate that it is at least one of them. The increase in States' implementing activities resulting from these factors contrasts starkly with States' responses (or rather the lack thereof) to earlier hard obligations in a number of treaties on international crimes, including the Genocide Convention, the Geneva Conventions, and the Torture Convention. See, generally, J.K. Kleffner, 'The Impact of Complementarity on National Implementation of Substantive International Criminal Law', 1 *J of Intl Crim Justice* (2003), 86.

This is not to suggest that the effects of complementarity as an incentive for the adoption of implementing legislation can be fully equated with its aptitude also to induce the actual enforcement of these laws.[5] The congruence lies in the possibility, however, that in both fields – implementation and enforcement – complementarity generates a pull-effect towards compliance as a mechanism of 'vertical domestication', whereby the norms embodied in the Rome Statute become incorporated into domestic legal systems and political processes.[6] This incorporation may culminate in core crimes being investigated and prosecuted domestically.

Beyond this generality, more specific features of the *formal framework of complementarity* further support its potential role as a catalyst for States' compliance with their obligation to investigate and prosecute.

First, the procedural setting of complementarity[7] contains elements of an *interaction* between the Court and national criminal jurisdictions, which may serve to induce States to carry out investigations and prosecutions. The starting-point for such interaction is the notification procedure under Article 18, paragraph 1, followed by the back-and-forth between the Prosecutor and States requesting a deferral, which is moderated by and conducted in front of the Pre-Trial Chamber or Trial Chamber and, in case of appeal, the Appeals Chamber.

Secondly, initiating an investigation or prosecution is insufficient for a State to invoke complementarity and to challenge admissibility successfully. Rather, in so doing, a State also has to satisfy the criteria of willingness and ability, which are applied independently by the Court and reviewed by it throughout the duration of the national proceedings. In so doing, the Court fulfils a *supervisory function*.

This supervision includes the review by the Prosecutor of the deferral to a State's investigation[8] or of a decision of inadmissibility;[9] the possibility

---

[5] That the enforcement of laws is something quite different from their adoption is illustrated, among other things, by the fact that the few implementing laws concerning international crimes prior to the ICC Statute had only been applied very rarely.

[6] See, generally, the writings of H.H. Koh, in particular H.H. Koh, 'Transnational Public Law Litigation', 100 *Yale L J* (1991), 2347; H.H. Koh, 'Transnational Legal Process', 75 *Nebraska L R* (1996), 181; H.H. Koh, 'The 1998 Frankel Lecture: Bringing International Law Home', 35 *Houston L R* (1998), 623.

[7] Rome Statute (n. 2) Arts. 15, 18, 19, 53; Rules (n. 3) Rules 48, 51-62, 133.

[8] Rome Statute (n. 2) Art. 18 para. 3.

[9] Ibid. Art. 19 para. 10.

for him to request the State to whose investigation he has deferred to inform him of the progress of its investigations and any subsequent prosecutions;[10] and his power to apply to the Pre-Trial Chamber for authorization of an investigation if, in his opinion, the review reveals that the complementarity threshold has been met.[11]

The most direct catalyst function resulting from this supervisory role is that it potentially induces States to attempt to conduct proceedings which satisfy the criteria of willingness and, to the extent that it is in their control, ability. A further, more subtle catalysing effect may be that a declaration of inadmissibility also endows national proceedings with a certain legitimacy. By holding a given State willing and able, national proceedings may be said to be less susceptible to allegations of bias.[12]

Together, the interactive and supervisory elements of the formal framework of complementarity suggest that the latter can at least in part be embedded into a managerial model of compliance.[13] Complementarity establishes a legal framework for the participation and engagement of States in the process of determining admissibility and in monitoring their investigations and prosecutions.

While the foregoing demonstrates that the formal framework of complementarity includes elements that support its conceptualization as a catalyst for compliance, one cannot fail to note the *limitations* inherent in that framework. Examples are an abusive invocation of complementarity, its potential to affect negatively the efficiency of ICC proceedings and to result in alleged perpetrators being warned, evidence being destroyed, etc. Many have already pointed out these problems,[14] and it would be difficult

---

[10] Ibid. Art. 18 para. 5; Art. 19 para. 11.

[11] Rules (n. 3) Rule 56 para. 1.

[12] This last aspect of complementarity's supervisory function as a vehicle for legitimacy needs to be approached with caution, however. There are instances in which flaws in national proceedings do not amount to unwillingness or inability. One important such gap results from the neglect of the complementarity requirements for the fair trial of an accused. The substance of complementarity would seem to provide only very limited room, if any, for the ICC to assume jurisdiction in cases where there have been violations of norms of due process, which work to the disadvantage of the person concerned.

[13] On the managerial theory of compliance, see, generally, A. Chayes and A. Handler Chayes, *The New Sovereignty: Compliance with International Regulatory Agreements* (Cambridge MA, Harvard University Press 1995).

[14] See, e.g., J.T. Holmes, 'The Principle of Complementarity', in R.S. Lee (ed.), *The International Criminal Court – The Making of the Rome Statute: Issues, Negotiations, Re-*

to add anything original to the analysis at this point in time. Instead, in the following we will identify limitations, which stem from other facets of the formal framework of complementarity and which are likely to create restrictions on its potential to serve as a catalyst for compliance.

The first such limitation is that the formal framework of complementarity encapsulates a relationship between national criminal jurisdictions and the ICC, which is to a large extent characterized by *antagonism*. States are assumed to be eager, in principle, to retain jurisdiction over cases, while the ICC is perceived as a threat to sovereignty. In turn, States are expected to investigate and prosecute because they want to bar the ICC from getting involved. They want to avoid the embarrassment that a declaration of admissibility would entail. States and the Prosecutor will compete for jurisdiction over a given case, with the former 'challenging' admissibility and the two parties litigating the matter before the Court.

Such an antagonistic relationship may in fact arise, especially regarding cases in which States had earlier made a conscious decision to remain inactive or regarding the majority of cases of '*unwillingness*' in the sense of Article 17, paragraph 2. In these scenarios, it may indeed be the threat by the ICC to consider matters of admissibility, which leads to a changed attitude on behalf of the State concerned. This could be the case where the reputational costs that a declaration of admissibility would entail, as well as the 'sanction' for non-compliance of forfeiting the right to exercise jurisdiction over a given case, outweighed the (political or other) costs of conducting investigations and prosecutions.[15] Such a sanctionist con-

---

sults (The Hague, Kluwer Law International 1999) 41, 76; D. Stoelting, 'ICC PreTrial Proceedings: Avoiding Gridlock', 9 *ILSA J of Intl and Comparative L* (2003), 413, 420-22; D. Cassel, 'The Rome Treaty for an International Criminal Court: A Flawed but Essential First Step', 6 *Brown J of World Affairs* (1999), 41, 48; P. Benvenuti, 'Complementarity of the International Criminal Court to National Criminal Jurisdictions', in F. Lattanzi and W. Schabas (eds.), *Essays on the Rome Statute of the International Criminal Court*, Vol. 1 (Il Sirente Ripa Fagnano Alto 1999) 21, 47; R. Dicker and H. Duffy, 'National Courts and the ICC', 6 *Brown J of World Affairs* (1999), 53, 59-60; G. Turone, 'Powers and Duties of the Prosecutor', in A. Cassese, P. Gaeta and J. Jones (eds.), *The Rome Statute of the International Criminal Court: A Commentary* (Oxford, Oxford University Press 2002) 1137, 1163.

[15] For a more elaborate work on such a model of compliance, see A.T. Guzman, 'International Law: A Compliance Based Theory', *U California Berkeley Public Law Research Paper* No. 47 (2001) <http://papers.ssrn.com/sol3/papers.cfm?abstract_id=260257> (21 July 2005).

ceptualization nevertheless reflects a somewhat limited view with regard to other potential scenarios.

One fails to see, for instance, how the threat of a declaration of '*inability*' may have similar effects, if, as will regularly be the case, inability is beyond the control of States.[16] Moreover, it would seem perfectly conceivable, for instance, that a State whose judicial system has collapsed seeks the assistance of the ICC in its efforts to rebuild that system and to prosecute perpetrators. Or a State may be willing to bring perpetrators to account but seeks to do so by having the ICC adjudicate a (number of) particularly sensitive case(s), thus paving the way for less sensitive cases to be investigated and prosecuted by national authorities.[17] Another reason for such a decision in these sensitive cases could be to prevent perceptions of bias, which a trial before the given State's domestic courts may provoke. The Court could play an important role in these situations, in which its relationship with national criminal jurisdictions would resemble more one of an 'affectionate partnership' than an 'ugly divorce'. And yet, such scenarios do not seem to have been in the minds of the drafters of the Rome Statute.

The 'antagonist assumption' of the formal framework of complementarity also entails that complementarity's catalyst function is limited to the extent to which the respective interests of States and the ICC to retain or assume jurisdiction over a case coincide. Only if both the Prosecutor *and* the State concerned intend to investigate a given (number of) case(s) will complementarity be able to serve to induce compliance by a national criminal jurisdiction. Lacking such concurrence, however, the pressure on States resulting from the threat of the ICC taking over a case cannot materialize. Given that the Court's ability will be limited to only a fraction of cases in

---

[16] This will most likely be the case for the explicitly mentioned forms of inability of 'a total or substantial collapse … of [a State's] national judicial system [due to which] the State is unable to obtain the accused or the necessary evidence and testimony or otherwise unable to carry out its proceedings'. Rome Statute (n. 2) Art. 17 para. 3. Other forms of inability may, however, very well be under the control of States. One such form is the lack of implementing legislation, which causes the 'unavailability' of a State's national judicial system. See also, Kleffner (n. 4).

[17] Such cases transferred to the ICC could, for instance, involve leaders of parties to an internal armed conflict or others exerting a large amount of power over organizations involved in the commission of core crimes.

each situation, the catalyst effects stemming from the formal framework of complementarity can thus reasonably be expected to be limited.[18]

While the formal framework of complementarity thus bears inherent limitations for it to function as a catalyst for compliance, one can currently observe a process of refinement and broadening of that function in the emerging *practice of the Court*, and centrally within it the Office of the Prosecutor.

Since his election, the ICC Prosecutor, Luis Moreno Ocampo, has stressed the catalyst function of complementarity. In his words during his first address to the Assembly of States Parties on 22 April 2003:

'The principle of complementarity established by the Statute compels the prosecutor's office to collaborate with national jurisdictions in order to help them improve their efficiency.

That is the first task of the prosecutor's office: make its best effort to help national jurisdictions fulfil their mission.

The prosecutor's office can do this in different ways. In a cooperative way, by giving the state the information received from different public sources or providing the state's personnel with training and technical support.

Also, due to the dissuasive effect that the mere existence of the court generates, the possibility of presenting a case at the International Criminal Court could convince some states with serious conflicts to take the appropriate action. ...

The efficiency of the International Criminal Court should not be measured by the number of cases that reach the court or by the content of its decisions. Quite on the contrary, because of the exceptional character of this institution, the absence of trials led by this court as a consequence of the regular functioning of national institutions, would be its major success.'[19]

---

[18] For the additional limitation stemming from the prosecutorial policy to investigate and prosecute only 'those who bear the greatest responsibility', see s. 2.

[19] ICC Press Release, 'OTP—Election of the Prosecutor, Statement by Mr. Moreno Ocampo' (2 May 2003) <http://www.icc-cpi.int/press/pressreleases/5.html> (11 August 2005). Similar statements were made subsequently, e.g., during the Ceremony for the Solemn Undertaking of the Chief Prosecutor on 16 June 2003. ICC Office of the Prosecutor, 'Paper on Some Policy Issues before the Office of the Prosecutor' (Policy Paper) 3-5 (2003) <http://www.icc-cpi.int/library/organs/otp/030905_Policy_Paper.pdf> (21 July 2005); ICC Office of the Prosecutor, 'Informal Expert Paper: The Principle of Complementarity in Practice' (Informal Expert Paper) (2003) 3 <http://www.icc-cpi.int/library/organs/otp/comple mentarity.pdf> (21 July 2005).

It is the declared policy of the Office of the Prosecutor that '[a] major part of the external relations and outreach strategy of the Office of the Prosecutor will be to encourage and facilitate States to carry out their primary responsibility of investigating and prosecuting crimes.'[20] To that end, '[t]he Office will develop formal and informal networks of contacts to encourage States to undertake State action, using means appropriate in the particular circumstances of a given case.'[21]

These statements reflect that the Office of the Prosecutor intends to make complementarity a central part of its overall policy and to use it proactively. In so doing, the Office goes beyond the antagonist assumption of the formal framework governing complementarity with a view to strengthening the latter's function as a catalyst for States to investigate and prosecute the core international crimes. In as much as the latter is understood not only as encapsulating the idea of pressuring States into investigating and prosecuting core crimes, but also as facilitating and assisting States in doing so, the Office of the Prosecutor is developing what can be described as 'positive complementarity'.[22]

The emergence of this broader understanding of complementarity as a catalyst for compliance suggests that complementarity gradually takes on a life on its own.[23] This 'life beyond the formal framework' also manifests itself in the organizational set-up of the Office of the Prosecutor, with one

---

[20] Policy Paper (n. 19) 5.

[21] Ibid.

[22] The ICC Prosecutor has described this positive approach to complementarity as one of the key strategic decisions guiding the work of his Office; see *Statement of the Prosecutor Luis Moreno Ocampo to Diplomatic Corps*, The Hague, Netherlands, 12 February 2004 <http://www.icc-cpi.int/library/organs/otp/OTP.SM20040212-EN.pdf> (12 August 2005).

[23] In fact, one might argue that the term 'complementarity' is wrongly employed in this context because it is not covered by the express terms of the Rome Statute relating to complementarity and should thus be called differently. However, I do not share this view. The complementary nature of the ICC rests on the fundamental premise that national jurisdictions remain the primary line of defense in the fight against impunity. Their strengthening should thus be understood as an integral part of effectuating complementarity with a view to achieving the object and purpose of the Statute, that is 'to put an end to impunity for the perpetrators of these crimes and thus to contribute to the prevention of such crimes'. Rome Statute (n. 2) preamble para. 5. For this reason, the term 'complementarity' will be employed in the following as encapsulating not only the formal framework but also the broader notion developed by the Office of the Prosecutor.

of its three Divisions, the Jurisdiction, Complementarity and Cooperation Division, being tasked with, amongst other things, the implementation of complementarity's catalyst function.[24] It is further affirmed in the current programme budget of the Court, which is based on the working assumption of a well functioning complementarity regime in the sense of the policy of the Office of the Prosecutor.[25]

The development of 'positive complementarity' and other features of the Prosecutor's evolving policy is, however, subject to the condition that they find a *basis in law*. This is not to suggest that the Prosecutor and his Office, in implementing and operationalizing the catalyst function of complementarity, is barred from assuming roles, which are not *expressly* provided for in the Rome Statute or the Rules of Procedure and Evidence.[26] To the extent that they are not, however, they must be either implied in the powers expressly assigned by the Statute or subsequently attributed as cus-

---

[24] The other two Divisions are the Investigation Division and the Prosecution Division.

[25] See Programme budget for 2004 and related documents, ICC-ASP/2/10, 'Draft programme budget for 2004 prepared by the Registrar', previously issued as ICC-ASP/2/2. The programme budget was drawn up with the view to enable the Office of the Prosecutor, *inter alia*, 'to engage in professional and constructive dialogue with States as required by the complementarity regime of the Rome Statute' (para 46). The Programme budget, para 52, further noted:

'[The Office] must have the capacity to obtain and analyse general background information from any source on the situation in crisis countries where there is an armed conflict and war crimes are being committed; on what the response of the national criminal justice system to such crimes is; and on what the international community and individual States are doing to assist the authorities of the country in crisis to respond adequately to the situation and the crimes [because w]ithout such capacity, the Office of the Prosecutor cannot give full effect to the complementarity regime of the Rome Statute or make its decisions on a sufficiently reliable factual basis. A responsible complementarity policy of the Office of the Prosecutor requires an analytical capacity to monitor relevant crises in a timely manner. Only if there is detection sufficiently early on of internal structures, processes and problems within a State which make it seem possible that war crimes are committed, can the Office of the Prosecutor contribute to the provision of effective assistance to the criminal justice system of that country, or use other instruments at its disposal as appropriate.'

See also paras. 69 ('external relations activities as required by the complementarity regime'), 75, and 79-81. The budget was adopted by Resolution ICC-ASP/2/Res.1 at the 5th plenary meeting on 12 September 2003 by consensus.

[26] Rules (n. 3).

tomary powers.[27] While it may be too early to speak of customary powers with regard to the powers of the Office of the Prosecutor, the doctrine of *implied powers* would appear to be of vital importance to determining the legal limits of the Office of the Prosecutor in operationalizing 'positive complementarity'.[28]

In sum, while both are subject to certain limitations, the formal framework and the emerging practice of the Office of the Prosecutor regarding complementarity suggest that complementarity serves as a mechanism to encourage and facilitate the compliance of States with their obligation to investigate and prosecute the core international crimes.

2.   DETERMINANTS INFLUENCING COMPLEMENTARITY'S CATALYST FUNCTION

The ability of complementarity to fulfil its function as a catalyst for compliance is and will be influenced by a variety of determinants. To a significant extent, these determinants are situation- or case-specific[29] and it would be futile to attempt to imagine all possible future scenarios. Furthermore, given the scant empirical data in relation to complementarity – the absence of the

---

[27] On the distinction between implied and customary powers, see H.G. Schermers and N, Blokker, *International Institutional Law: Unity within Diversity*, 4th edn. (Leiden, Martinus Nijhoff Publishers 2004) 176 para. 232.

[28] It is acknowledged that it may nevertheless be difficult to determine the extent of the powers implied, not the least because the process of determining implied powers (Can they derive only from explicit powers or also from purposes and functions of organizations? Must they be necessary or essential for the organization to perform its functions and, if so, what is actually 'necessary' or 'essential'?) is characterized by a good degree of uncertainty and inconsistencies. See ibid. 177 para. 233.

[29] The distinction between 'situations' and 'cases' is understood here as the former referring to a larger set of circumstances and the latter to circumstances in which an individual suspect has been identified. For that distinction and its relevance for different stages of admissibility proceedings, see, *inter alia*, H. Olásolo, 'The Prosecutor of the ICC before the Initiation of Investigations: A Quasi-Judicial or a Political Body', 3 *Intl Crim L R* (2003), 87, 99-100; H. Friman, 'Investigation and Prosecution', in R.S. Lee (ed.), *The International Criminal Court: Elements of Crimes and Rules of Procedure and Evidence* (New York, Transnational Publishers 2001) 494.

formal opening of an investigation by the Prosecutor,[30] of any ruling by the Court, and of the invocation of any of the provisions on complementarity by parties to the proceedings before the Court – it would be premature to attempt to draw any definite conclusions on the basis of past 'experiences'.

Rather, at this early stage of the Court's functioning, it appears more useful to hypothesize about the most obvious of these determinants, which can be extracted (at least partly) from the evolving operationalization of complementarity in practice. This evolving practice supplies some early examples, which may serve to illustrate the influence that given determinants exert on complementarity's impact on national repression, and thus bears the potential of moving our analysis beyond mere speculation.

Such a preliminary analysis of the respective determinants could serve as the first step in a continuous process of gathering and analysing determinants, with a view to determining whether and to what extent they have a bearing on complementarity's catalyst function.[31] In the long-term, such a process could then contribute to the development of a template of determinants, which provides an analytical tool for evaluating past strategies, as well as planning and predicting the effect of future strategies, to fulfil complementarity's function as a catalyst for compliance.[32]

For analytical purposes, one can distinguish between determinants that influence complementarity's ability to fulfil its catalyst function because they *generate* an impact, on the one hand, and those that do so because they determine whether and to what extent the impact is *received,* on the other hand. However, this distinction should not be misunderstood to suggest that the two elements of impact-generation and impact-reception exist in isolation from each other. Quite to the contrary, it is their interaction and mutual dependence which makes them worthy of analysis for our purposes. For the same reason, the two elements should not be conceived of as static,

---

[30] Note that the statements by the Prosecutor that he is closely following the situation in the DRC did not constitute the formal start of an investigation. Nor did the referrals of the situations by the DRC and Uganda. These are only the first step, which may ultimately *lead* to the opening of an investigation after the determination of a 'reasonable basis', which, in turn, includes considerations of complementarity. Compare Rome Statute (n. 2) Art. 53 para. 1b and Rules (n. 3) Rule 48.

[31] On assessing the causality (or lack thereof) between the various determinants and a possible impact on national repression, see s. 3.

[32] On the need for such a template, see Informal Expert Paper (n. 19) 5 fn 2.

as they may evolve over time in a given situation or case.[33] The catalyst function of complementarity needs to be understood in terms of a process rather than a singular event.

The first determinant is the *disposition* of the impact recipient or addressee, that is a given targeted State and its national criminal jurisdiction. Whether a given State is 'unwilling' or 'unable' will have significant bearing on whether and how complementarity can serve as a catalyst for compliance. In the former case, complementarity's catalyst function will depend on whether or not a successful strategy can be employed through which the State will be 'convinced' or pressured into conducting genuine investigations and prosecutions. In the case of inability, however, such pressure will often be superfluous due to the collapse or unavailability of a judicial system. Whether and to what extent complementarity can function as a catalyst for compliance in such a situation will be determined by its contribution to the facilitation of and assistance to the affected State.

In addition to this general distinction between 'unwilling' and 'unable' States, the underlying, case-specific *causes* of the disposition will have to be taken into account as a second set of determinants of complementarity's catalyst role.[34] Consider, for instance, a situation in which the problems of national enforcement stem from the fact that a limited number of prominent and powerful individuals opposed to the State exert negative influence on

---

[33] For example, a given complementarity strategy targeting the executive and/or legislative authorities of a State may have yielded the revocation of an amnesty law, which had previously barred national judicial organs from acting, thus making them 'unable' in the sense of Art. 17 para. 3 of the Rome Statute (n. 2). After the revocation of the de jure amnesty, the judicial authorities may seek to shield the alleged perpetrators; see Rome Statute (n. 2) Art. 17 para. 2. The complementarity strategy employed for overcoming the unwillingness of these authorities may be different from the one which resulted in the revocation of the amnesty law. Another example would be the situation in which complementarity, understood in the broad sense by the Prosecutor, has contributed to overcoming the collapse of a State's judicial system by galvanizing efforts of States and other actors to rebuild that system, but then facing proceedings, which 'are not being conducted independently or impartially, and ... in a manner which, in the circumstances, is inconsistent with an intent to bring the person concerned to justice'. Rome Statute (n. 2) Art. 17 para. 2c.

[34] See M. Morris, 'Complementarity and its Discontents: States, Victims, and the International Criminal Court', in D. Shelton, *International Crimes, Peace, and Human Rights: The Role of the International Criminal Court* (New York, Transnational Publishers 2000) 177, 183-88.

national investigative, prosecutorial and adjudicative authorities in a certain region. Here, a positive impact can be realized by a consensual division of labour through which the transferral of these persons to The Hague can pave the way for investigating and prosecuting less prominent and powerful persons (and thus, less politically sensitive cases) domestically.

The way in which complementarity can fulfil its catalyst function in the aforementioned example differs starkly from a situation in which 'inability' results from the destruction of court buildings during armed conflict and the flight of members of the judiciary from the fighting. Under these circumstances, complementarity, understood in the broad sense suggested by the Prosecutor,[35] would have to be operationalized as part of a broader effort to generate financial support for the rebuilding of the judicial infrastructure and to create incentives for the voluntary repatriation of those displaced, for instance by cooperating with the UNHCR, after the conflict has ended. The catalyst function of complementarity may then more likely lie in identifying the inability of a national criminal jurisdiction, drawing attention to it and thereby putting other actors, such as intergovernmental organizations (IGOs), non-governmental organizations (NGOs) and individual States, on notice that their support is needed in order to reinvigorate the national judicial system concerned.

In short, the effects of complementarity as a catalyst for compliance and the strategies that are needed in order to fulfil such a role depend to a significant degree on the factual situation underlying issues of admissibility.

Closely connected to the causes for the disposition of a given State, which give rise to 'unwillingness' or 'inability', is the question of *which national institution(s)* is/are primarily responsible for impunity. As a third determinant, an answer to this question will ascertain who needs to be the object of complementarity as a catalyst for compliance.

The formal framework of complementarity treats the State as a monolithic entity, subjecting the 'State' as a whole to the complementarity assessment without differentiating between its component branches – legislative, executive and judicial. Yet, reality is often more complex. If, for example, a blanket amnesty is granted by the executive or the legislature, which thereby 'decides not to prosecute'[36] 'for the purpose of shielding the

---

[35] S. 1.
[36] Cf., Rome Statute (n. 2) Art. 17 para. 1b and Art. 17 para. 2a.

person[s] concerned from criminal responsibility',[37] it is conceivable that the judiciary remains *willing* to investigate and prosecute. Rather, judicial organs would be *unable* to proceed with an investigation and prosecution because, as a matter of national law, they have to apply the amnesty. Being 'unwilling' or 'unable' are thus neither mutually exclusive notions – a *State* may be both at the same time – nor can a State hide behind the positive attitude of one organ when another such organ satisfies the admissibility criteria.

In order to operationalize complementarity as a catalyst for compliance in a given situation, it will often be necessary to look behind the veil of the State and identify specific branches of government and, indeed, specific State organs, such as a given court, prosecutorial office or investigative unit, and to develop different complementarity strategies with regard to each of them.

The fourth determinant, which is likely to influence whether and to what extent complementarity can fulfil its catalyst function, is the *prosecutorial strategy* and *actual operationalization of complementarity by the Office of the Prosecutor*.

As far as *prosecutorial strategy* is concerned, several statements by the Prosecutor and the 'Paper on Some Policy Issues before the Office of the Prosecutor' indicate that, as a general rule, the focus will be on prosecuting *'those who bear the greatest responsibility, such as the leaders of the State or organisation allegedly responsible for those [core] crimes.'*[38] This approach may be necessitated by the logistical and resource-related constraints of the ICC. However, it also further limits the potential of complementarity to fulfil a catalyst function if the general assumption of the formal framework – an antagonist relationship between 'unwilling' States and the Prosecutor – materializes.[39] For, such a prosecutorial strategy entails that the pressure on States, which results from the threat of the ICC taking over from these unwilling States, is limited to 'those who bear the greatest responsibility'. The 'unwilling' State could safely assume that all other indi-

---

[37] Cf., ibid. Art. 17 para. 1b and Art. 17 para. 2a.
[38] Policy Paper (n. 19) 3, 7.
[39] Cf., s. 1.

viduals, who fall outside that category, are beyond the reach of the ICC and could thus benefit from impunity.[40]

It may therefore be asked whether a more tacit prosecutorial strategy may not be more apt to maximize complementarity's effectiveness as a catalyst for compliance in situations of 'unwilling' States. Naturally, such an alternative approach would not overcome the logistical and resource related constraints alluded to. It would not alter the Court's capacity to deal with only a limited number of cases. And yet, the *possibility,* even if only theoretical, that cases involving all categories of perpetrators are eligible for an admissibility determination by the Court may enhance the pressure on States to prosecute such cases themselves.

Moreover, the problem of an express limitation to 'those who bear the greatest responsibility' is not confined to cases of 'unwilling' States, which seek to bar the ICC from taking action. The Ugandan referral provides an ample illustration of the role of this prosecutorial policy of the Office of the Prosecutor as a determinant of complementarity's ability to fulfil its catalyst function in other cases.

The 2000 Ugandan Amnesty Act granted amnesty to 'any Ugandan who has at any time since the 26th day of January, 1986 engaged in or is engaging in war or armed rebellion against the government of the Republic of Uganda'.[41] The Act provides that these persons 'shall not be prosecuted or subjected to any form of punishment for the participation in the war or rebellion for any crime committed in the cause of the war or armed rebellion'.[42] The amnesty thus extended to crimes within the jurisdiction of the ICC.

The permissibility of such amnesties for ICC crimes is at least doubtful if one considers the legal regime pre-existing the ICC Statute and the ad-

---

[40] It may be added that such a prosecutorial strategy also entails the creation of an additional, unwritten hurdle to admissibility because suspects may raise their low-ranking status as a bar to action by the ICC. Such arguments could be based on the reasonable expectation created by the Office of the Prosecutor and could then take forms similar to what one can now witness before the Special Court for Sierra Leone, which is statutorily limited to 'those who bear the greatest responsibility', Statute of the Special Court for Sierra Leone, Art. 1 para. 1.

[41] Uganda Amnesty Act (2000) pt II para. 3(1) <http://www.c-r.org/accord/uganda/accord11/downloads/2000_Jan_The_Amnesty_Act.doc> (21 July 2005).

[42] Ibid. pt II para. 3(2).

missibility criteria in Article 17 of the Statute.[43] It may therefore come as no surprise that, according to a Press Release of early 2004 announcing that the Ugandan President 'took the decision to refer the situation concerning the Lord's Resistance Army to the Prosecutor of the International Criminal Court[, …] President Museveni indicated to the Prosecutor his intention to amend [the] amnesty [Act].'[44] However, the express aim of the amendment was 'to exclude the leadership of the LRA, ensuring that those bearing the greatest responsibility for the crimes against humanity committed in Northern Uganda are brought to justice.'[45] In other words, the prosecutorial policy of limiting the action of the Office of the Prosecutor to a certain category of individuals found reflection in the amendment of the Amnesty Act, thus equally limiting the scope of national investigations and prosecutions to these persons. If the amendment were adopted in the proposed form, only 'those bearing the greatest responsibility' would be excluded from the amnesty. All others, however, would still be able to invoke it before Ugandan courts and would not be investigated and prosecuted by the ICC Prosecutor in accordance with his prosecutorial strategy.

A further aspect of the current prosecutorial strategy as a determinant of how complementarity's catalyst function can be fulfilled is that the Office of the Prosecutor is to take action *only where there is a clear case of failure to take national action*.[46] If the two situations, which have so far reached the public domain – the Democratic Republic of Congo (DRC) and Uganda – are anything to go by, this policy entails that situations will be targeted in which 'inability' plays a much more prominent role than 'unwillingness'. Naturally, this might be different in other situations.[47] The relevant point for our analysis remains, however, that the two mentioned situations are characterized by systemic, situation-wide challenges to effective national

---

[43] See, among others, the contribution to this roundtable by Claudia Cárdenas Aravena.

[44] ICC Press Release, 'President of Uganda refers situation concerning the Lord's Resistance Army (LRA) to the ICC' (29 January 2004) No. pids.001.2004-EN <http://www.icc-cpi.int/pressrelease_details&id=16.html> (21 July 2005).

[45] Ibid.

[46] Policy Paper (n. 19) 5.

[47] Ibid. The Prosecutor recognizes this by limiting this 'general rule' to 'the initial phase' of the operations of the OTP.

investigations and prosecutions, such as the absence of judicial infrastructure.[48]

Both Uganda and the DRC have sought the assistance of the ICC in their
efforts to combat impunity and have referred the situations to the ICC themselves *(auto-referral)*. These situations thus call for an operationalization
of complementarity, which differs considerably from strategies in situations where the challenge consists, for instance, of overcoming the shielding of one particular individual or group of individuals. The complementarity
strategy of the OTP would in all likelihood be more directed towards serving as a catalyst for assisting the State concerned in (re-)building its national judicial system.

Both of the aforementioned elements of the prosecutorial policy of the
Office of the Prosecutor (the limitations to those individuals who bear the
greatest responsibility and to situations of clear failure of national authorities to act) entail that many cases of core crimes, which have occurred in a
given situation, will remain unaddressed by the Court and the domestic
legal system of the territorial State, thus leaving what has been referred to
as the 'impunity gap'.[49] This gap has been recognized by the Office of the
Prosecutor and has been integrated into his model of complementarity understood in the broader sense referred to above.[50]

An important aspect of the prosecutorial strategy and the actual operationalization of complementarity influencing its ability to fulfil its function
as a catalyst for compliance is, in turn, *how the impunity gap will be
addressed*.

Given the legal and practical restraints facing the ICC, it seems unlikely
that the Court will provide (a portion of) the required resources for rebuilding a national judicial system. This would meet not only the objection that

---

[48] On the situation in Ituri, see, e.g., Interim Report of the Special Rapporteur on the
Situation of Human Rights in the Democratic Republic of the Congo UN Doc. A/58/534 (24
October 2003) para. 69. On the situation in northern Uganda, see, e.g., Ugandan Ministry of
Finance, Planning and Economic Development Office of the Prime Minister and Office of
the President 'Post-Conflict Reconstruction: The Case of Northern Uganda Discussion Paper 7 (Draft)' (April 2003) 10 <http://www.finance.go.ug/events/FINAL%20CG%20Draft
%20on%20Northern%20Uganda%5B1%5D.doc> (21 July 2005).

[49] Policy Paper (n. 19) 7.

[50] S. 1. For the reflection of the 'impunity gap' in the policy of the Prosecutor, see
Policy Paper (n. 19).

it depleted the scarce resources available to the Court to fulfil its core functions, but also the legal objection that it goes beyond the mandate given to the Court by the Statute.[51] However, a number of other measures by the Office of the Prosecutor would seem to meet with neither of these objections.

Thus, the Office of the Prosecutor may publicly announce that a given State's national judicial system meets prima facie the admissibility threshold of being 'unable' genuinely to investigate and prosecute core crimes.[52] Such a public announcement highlights the need for judicial reform and reconstruction and, in turn, may support, or indeed trigger, actions by other international actors, such as IGOs, NGOs and individual States, to render assistance to that State. Rather than assuming that role itself, the OTP would thus 'flag' a given situation as meriting the support of the international community.[53]

Beyond interactions resulting from such situation-specific announcements, relationships between the OTP and relevant actors can further be fostered by regular exchanges, through which information is shared and plans of action developed with a view to strengthening and supporting national judicial systems in their efforts to bring perpetrators of core crimes to justice.[54]

---

[51] Note that the Programme budget (n. 25) does not foresee any expenditure for assisting States in rebuilding their national judicial systems.

[52] See, e.g., in the case of the DRC, ICC Press Release, 'Communications Received by the Office of the Prosecutor of the ICC', s. III (16 July 2003) No.: pids.009.2003-EN <http://www.icc-cpi.int/library/press/mediaalert/16_july__english.pdf> (21 July 2005).

[53] The announcement about the DRC, for instance, may have contributed to or at least strengthened a number of initiatives. See, e.g., 'Fifteenth Report of the Secretary-General on the United Nations Organization Mission in the Democratic Republic of the Congo', 7-8 paras 27, 29-30 UN Doc. S/2004/251, referring to French and EU assistance in rebuilding judicial infrastructure and UN support in that respect. See also 'Report on the Situation of Human Rights in the Democratic Republic of the Congo, submitted by the Special Rapporteur, Ms. Iulia Motoc', para. 71 UN Doc. E/CN.4/2004/34 (10 March 2005), noting that 'the judicial system in Ituri is now operational'. It is acknowledged, however, that a causality between these initiatives and the public announcement by the OTP may not be proven, see s. 3.

[54] See, e.g., the *Vancouver Dialogue*, which seeks to bring together the experience, expertise and resources of institutions, governments, civil society and funding organizations involved in international justice. R. Adamson and A. Vamos-Goldman, 'The Expectation

A further measure, which bears the potential of contributing to supporting and strengthening national judicial systems is to recruit members of the
judiciary of the targeted State for ICC investigations and prosecutions.[55]
Certainly, such involvement has to be approached with the utmost care so
as not to recruit individuals who may compromise the investigations of the
OTP. However, with the necessary safeguards in place, such involvement –
besides enhancing the expertise of the OTP, the sense of ownership and
perceived legitimacy of investigations by the respective society—will increase the expertise of members of the local judiciary in questions of international criminal law. Upon returning to their State, the latter may function
as multipliers of such expertise by sharing their experiences with col-
leagues.[56]

One can conclude from the foregoing that a variety of factors determine
whether, to what extent and how complementarity can fulfil its catalyst
function to induce and facilitate genuine national investigations and prosecutions. A further analysis and refinement of these determinants may contribute to the development of effective complementarity strategies in a given
situation.

Gap: Summary of the First Meeting of the Vancouver Dialogue' (June 2003) <http://
www.gjp.ubc.ca/_media/act/ExpectationGapReport.pdf>. Possible strategies could take the
form of internationalizing national courts and linking them to the ICC in order to improve
capacity building. See also, Stanley Foundation, 'Creating the International Legal Assistance Consortium' (February 2000) <http://reports.stanleyfoundation.org/ILAC00p.pdf (21
July 2005). See further H. Strohmeyer, 'Collapse and Reconstruction of a Judicial System:
The United Nations Missions in Kosovo and East Timor', 95 *AJIL* (2001), 46, 62 (calling
for the UN to enhance its own capacity to establish a functioning judiciary as rapidly as
possible and suggesting to formulate a 'quick-start package', encompassing 'criminal procedure and criminal codes, as well as a code regulating the activities of the police' for transitional administrations).

[55] This has also been suggested in the Policy Paper (n. 19) 8-9. Since then, at least
one Congolese Magistrate is working in the OTP on the Congolese situation.

[56] For that purpose, the OTP has set up a Visiting Professionals Programme of the
Office of the Prosecutor, which aims to draw on the expertise of seasoned professionals in
areas relevant to the functions of the Office and to enhance the expertise of such candidates
in ways that would contribute towards a better understanding of the mission of the Office in
the candidate's professional community, thereby enhancing the effectiveness of the Office
and the Court as a whole. For a discription of the programme, see <http://www.icc-cpi.int/
otp/vpp.html> (21 July 2005).

3. THE IMPACT ON NATIONAL REPRESSION OF CORE CRIMES

The conceptualization of complementarity as a catalyst for compliance suggests that a chosen complementarity strategy needs to be assessed in light of whether and to what extent it impacts the national repression of the core crimes. One of the questions that arises in connection to such an evaluation is how the impact of a given complementarity strategy can be measured.

The development of a methodological framework for measuring the impact of (a given) complementarity (strategy) on national enforcement is a challenging task for a number of reasons. First, the idiosyncrasies of the ICC and (the operationalization) of complementarity make any attempt to draw analogies to the methodology of measuring the effects on national jurisdictions of international agreements, treaty regimes or international judicial bodies in other areas of international law an undertaking of questionable value. More fundamentally, however, even if one were to find such analogies because of similarities between the ICC and, for instance, other judicial bodies,[57] the lack of coherence in methodology for measuring the effects of such bodies would pose a second challenge.[58]

---

[57] One could attempt to search for such an analogy, for instance, in a methodology for measuring the effect on national jurisdictions of the rule requiring the exhaustion of local remedies before having access to international human rights bodies, which resembles, remotely as it might be, the principle of complementarity. For such resemblance, see A.A. Cancado Trindade, *The Application of the Rule of Exhaustion of Local Remedies in International Law: Its Rationale in the International Protection of Individual Rights* (Cambridge, Cambridge University Press 1983) 279-287. Cancado Trindade notes at 283, *inter alia*, that the 'close inter-relationship between the individual's duty of exhaustion and the State's duty to provide local remedies *illustrates a modern shift of emphasis towards improvement of national judicial systems of judicial protection*' (emphasis added). However, to the knowledge of the present author, no methodology exists for measuring the effect of the exhaustion of the local remedies rule on national jurisdictions.

[58] See, e.g., the contributions of various authors in T.M. Franck and G.H. Fox (eds.), *International Law Decisions in National Courts* (New York, Transnational Publishers 1996). None of those authors addresses the methodological question of how the effect of international law decisions can be measured beyond the truism that the reliance on decisions of international judicial bodies by national courts is an indicator of the former having an effect on the latter. See, e.g., S. Ordonez and D. Reilly, 'Effect of the Jurisprudence of the International Court of Justice on National Courts', in T.M. Franck and G.H. Fox 335-371. Ordonez and Reilly recognize the lack of an established analytical framework (344-345). However,

Thirdly, the situations in or between targeted States, in which com-plementarity is envisaged to operate, are very complex. Due to the nature of the crimes within the jurisdiction of the ICC, these situations are characterized by the turmoil entailed by armed conflicts, systematic or wide-spread attacks against the civilian population and the implementation of genocidal policies, as well as by the transition from such periods to more stable and peaceful situations. It may therefore prove difficult to overcome the problems stemming from the resulting lack of access to and reliability of information, which could provide the basis for an assessment of whether complementarity has had an effect.

A fourth and final challenge stems from the professional limitation of the present author, being educated as a lawyer rather than a (political) ana-lyst.

With these caveats in mind, the following tentative and general observa-tions may nevertheless be ventured.

The measuring of the impact of complementarity on national repression of the core crimes presupposes the identification of *indicators* to be used. The overall indicator can be derived from the aim of complementarity as a catalyst for compliance. If a given complementarity strategy causes an im-provement, in both quantitative and qualitative terms, in the targeted State's compliance with its obligation to investigate and prosecute the core crimes properly, such strategy will have worked.

The difficulty will probably lie, however, in proving that it was com-plementarity, rather than other factors, which *caused* the improvement. Complementarity will often function alongside other factors and actors, which may exert influence on national repression of the core crimes. In a

---

the effects of international judicial bodies do not exhaust themselves in the direct reliance on their jurisprudence. Thus, a condemnation by a regional or universal human rights body could, for instance, provoke the amendment of the national law which gave rise to the par-ticular violation of human rights or provoke the change of administrative practices, which led to the violation. The disagreement over the methodology to measure the effects of inter-national legal instruments is not limited to judicial bodies. See, e.g., in the area of human rights treaties, the differences in opinion, on the one hand, of O.A. Hathaway, 'Do Human Rights Treaties Make a Difference?', 111 *Yale L J* (2002), 1935, and, on the other hand, of R. Goodman and D. Jinks, 'Measuring the Effects of Human Rights Treaties', 14 *EJIL* (2003), 171. See also, Hathaway's response to the latter work: O.A. Hathaway, 'Testing Conven-tional Wisdom', 14 *EJIL* (2003), 185.

situation of internal armed conflict, which caused the collapse of the judicial infrastructure, for instance, the implementation of a complementarity strategy of the Office of the Prosecutor may coincide with the parties to the conflict implementing a peace agreement, which paves the way for the judicial authorities being able to operate again. It will then be difficult to establish conclusively a causal connection between (a given) complementarity (strategy) and a change in a national jurisdiction's willingness and/or ability to investigate and prosecute the core crimes. The understanding of 'complementarity' by the Office of the Prosecutor may also add to the complications in establishing such a causal connection, as it seems to encompass ideas that are similar, or in fact identical, to other notions, which may exert an influence on national repression but may function in isolation from the ICC.[59]

The converse dimension of the problem of causality is that the reason for a lack of improvement in national repression may very well lie outside complementarity. A myriad of factors may prevent the potential of a complementarity strategy from materializing[60] and the ultimate result of a situation worsening or at least not having improved may be *in spite* of rather than *because of* that strategy.

In addition to the problem of causality, the global formula 'quantitative and qualitative increase in investigation and prosecution = impact of complementarity' also obstructs the view on individual elements of a given complementarity strategy, which may or may not have worked. Complementarity strategies will have to be tailored, at least to some extent, to the specific situation at hand, taking into account the idiosyncratic causes

---

[59] For instance, 'complementarity' as a framework of assistance to States may exist alongside and overlap with assistance to States in the form of development aid from donor States, IGOs, such as the UNDP, and private donations with a view to rebuilding their judicial systems.

[60] An example would be a situation in which the targeted State authorities consider the costs of conducting investigations and prosecutions too high to outweigh the costs of a declaration of admissibility. See n. 15 and accompanying text. If the military in a given State openly threatens to overthrow a newly established, fragile transitional government and use force if members of the military accused of having committed core crimes are investigated and prosecuted, the government may decide to abstain from investigating and prosecuting, notwithstanding all efforts of the OTP to operationalize complementarity in support of genuine national investigations and prosecutions, which would otherwise have proven succesful.

for impunity. These causes may also require different responses to different composite organs of a State rather than to the State as a whole.[61] The development of situation-specific indicators may therefore be called for.

Thus, when the obstacle to national investigations and prosecutions stems from the shielding of an individual suspect by the prosecutorial authorities of a State, an obvious indicator of complementarity having had an impact would consist of these authorities abandoning their obstructionist attitude and paving the way for a trial. This differs from a situation of systemic impunity caused by the total or substantial collapse of a State's judicial system. Here, an indicator of complementarity's having fulfilled its catalyst function would consist of the actual rebuilding of the judicial infrastructure, to which the operationalization of complementarity by the Office of the Prosecutor has contributed.

Be that as it may, there are also a number of *direct indicators,* which leave no doubt that complementarity has impacted national repression of the core crimes. This is notably the case when investigative or prosecutorial organs or courts refer to it in the course of proceedings. Although examples are currently absent, it is conceivable that this may occur in a variety of ways.

One such way is for judicial organs to motivate their decision to investigate or prosecute by reference to complementarity, arguing that the latter reaffirms or imposes on them the obligation to assume jurisdiction. Another way could be for complementarity to be referred to as a legitimizing factor. For instance, a national court could invoke complementarity as an argument countering the claim (by an accused, another national authority or another State) that the ICC rather than a national jurisdiction should assume jurisdiction over the case at hand. Another example of complementarity being directly invoked as a legitimizing factor could occur when a national court uses the 'pedigree' of willingness and ability, which derives from a prior finding of inadmissibility by the ICC, in order to counter arguments that the national jurisdiction is unwilling or unable.[62]

It is acknowledged that these direct indicators may often be absent not least because, in 'clear case[s] of failure to take national action',[63] judicial

---

[61] See s. 2.

[62] Recall, however, that this has to be approached cautiously, see n. 12.

[63] See n. 46 and accompanying text.

organs will frequently be silent. The identification of more subtle indicators will therefore be necessary in order to assess the functioning of the Court and the operationalization of complementarity as a catalyst for compliance. Indeed, the formulation of 'performance indicators'[64] should be integrated into the development of complementarity strategies for a given situation. It would appear useful to draw upon the experiences in other fields[65] in seeking methodological guidance.

4.   CONCLUSION

Several aspects of complementarity, both formal and informal, suggest that it can be conceptualized as a catalyst for national criminal jurisdictions conducting genuine investigations and prosecutions of core crimes. As such, complementarity bears the potential of contributing to the gradual overcoming or at least mitigation of the challenges to effective national repression of these crimes.

However, the way in and extent to which complementarity will in actuality achieve its aim of doing so will depend to a large extent on its being operationalized flexibly, taking into account the idiosyncrasies of a given situation in which core crimes have been committed. An assessment and systematization of the determinants influencing the functioning of complementarity seems prudent with a view to developing situation-tailored complementarity strategies for new situations. Such strategies should be reviewed and refined constantly in order to maximize their positive impact on national criminal jurisdictions. In developing the framework of review, methodological questions of how the impact can be measured need to be addressed.

Last but not least it needs to be emphasized that the somewhat isolated approach adopted in the present contribution – focusing solely on complementarity as a catalyst of compliance – is not meant to suggest that other factors influencing the behaviour of States and their composite organs can

---

[64] Such indicators have been integrated into the Programme Budget with a view to assessing the performance of the various organs of the ICC.

[65] One could think of fields such as 'law and economics' and social impact assessments conducted with regard to operations of multilateral development banks.

be neglected. Complementarity is not the solution to all problems and persisting problems are not necessarily the result of a failed complementarity strategy. Achieving the goal of genuine national investigations and prosecutions will often require broader measures than simply effectuating a given complementarity strategy. A strengthening of the catalyst function of complementarity must go hand in hand with the enhancement of such measures.

COMMENTS ON CHAPTER 3 OF JANN KLEFFNER

Federica Gioia*

1. JANN KLEFFNER'S CORE ASSUMPTIONS: GENERAL REMARKS

I was asked by the organizers of this roundtable, whom I thank, to introduce and comment on Jann Kleffner's paper 'Complementarity as a Catalyst for Compliance', now chapter 3 in this book. I approached it both as a scholar and as an individual deeply interested in and committed to the success of the mandate of the International Criminal Court (ICC). I was not disappointed in either capacity.

As a scholar, I appreciated both the clarity of the presentation and the accuracy of the legal research supporting the views.

As an individual sincerely hoping that the ICC will achieve its ambitious objectives, I welcomed the assumption that the principle of complementarity, as the rules governing the relationship between the ICC and national jurisdictions are comprehensively referred to, should work as a 'catalyst for compliance'.

Jann Kleffner's core assumptions can be summarized as follows: Complementarity will work as a 'catalyst for compliance'. This is tantamount to saying that the very existence of complementarity is aimed at inducing and facilitating the compliance of States with their obligation to exercise criminal jurisdiction over those responsible for the most heinous crimes. Accordingly, complementarity will have an impact on national criminal jurisdictions and such impact will be one relevant factor, by no means a lesser one, by which the failure or success of the ICC as a whole will be ultimately measured.

---

* Dr. jur.; Legal Adviser, International Criminal Court. The views expressed in this chapter are solely those of the author.

J.K. Kleffner & G. Kor (eds.), Complementary Views on Complementarity
© 2006, T·M·C·ASSER PRESS, *The Hague, The Netherlands and the Authors*

I should like to point out at the outset that I subscribe to this three-pronged assumption. I would even go a step further, submitting that complementarity, as established and governed by the Rome Statute, *was meant* to have an impact on national criminal jurisdictions, or to serve as 'a catalyst for compliance'.

Several provisions of the Rome Statute seem to support this conclusion. I will focus on those which seem to be the most significant.

2.   THE STATES' OBLIGATIONS ACCORDING TO THE ROME STATUTE

A need and call for compliance by States is explicit and apparent in provisions such as Articles 86 and 88 of the Statute.

Article 86 establishes the States Parties' obligation to 'cooperate fully with the Court in its investigation and prosecution of crimes within the jurisdiction of the Court.'[1]

Article 88 sets forth a fundamental tenet of this general obligation by stating that 'States parties shall ensure that there are procedures available under their national law for all the forms of cooperation.'[2] These forms of cooperation are specified in Part 9 of the Rome Statute, entitled 'International Cooperation and Judicial Assistance'.

3.   THE NOTION OF 'INABILITY' OF A NATIONAL JUDICIAL SYSTEM

A further element of the Statute suitably construed as calling for compliance is embodied in the very notion of inability, that is one of the two forms, besides unwillingness, which triggers the jurisdiction of the Court under the principle of complementarity. The image most likely to come to mind when evoking the inability of a State is that of a failed State, that is a State suffering from instability or disorder, such as from a situation in which either no government exists or the government in place is unable to provide basic public order throughout the State territory or part of it.

---

[1]   Rome Statute of the International Criminal Court (Rome Statute) Art. 86 (adopted 17 July 1998, entered into force 1 July 2002) UN Doc. A/CONF.183/9.

[2]   Ibid. Art. 88.

Such a scenario does indeed belong to the notion of inability as expressed in the Rome Statute, namely as a 'total or substantial collapse or unavailability of its [a State's] national judicial system.'[3]

However, there is more to inability than the scenario of a collapsed State. The Statute provides that inability might also be triggered by the 'unavailability'[4] of a given legal system. What does unavailability amount to? It may be briefly described as a situation in which a legal system is theoretically in place and functioning as a whole but incapable of functioning in respect of a given case, due to legal or factual obstacles, and always provided that such unavailability results in the State being 'unable to obtain the accused or the necessary evidence and testimony or otherwise unable to carry out its proceedings.'[5]

Regarding obstacles of a legal nature, the issue is closely intertwined with the implementation of the Rome Statute. The term 'unavailability' might comprise not only lack of adequate procedures (due to the State's failure to honour the obligation set forth under Article 88 of the Rome Statute), but also the lack of adequate substantive provisions enabling a State to punish conduct falling within the scope of the ICC's jurisdiction under terms consistent with the Rome Statute. More specifically, the lack of proper implementation might amount to unavailability in case of either total absence of provisions criminalizing the crimes provided for in the Statute or of substantial discrepancies between the national legislation and the Statute liable to result in impunity. Both scenarios are likely to result in the Court assuming jurisdiction under the rule of complementarity.

As stated in Jann Kleffner's chapter, the Statute does not contain any express obligation for States to implement its substantive provisions. Nevertheless, an obligation to ensure substantive compliance with the Statute appears to be implicit in a number of affirmations of the Preamble to the Rome Statute: Paragraph 6 recalls 'the duty of every State to exercise its criminal jurisdiction over those responsible for international crimes'[6] while paragraph 4 stresses that the most serious international crimes 'must not go unpunished and that their effective prosecution must be ensured by taking

---

[3] Ibid. Art. 17 para. 3.
[4] Ibid.
[5] Ibid.
[6] Ibid. preamble para. 6.

measures at the national level and by enhancing international cooperation.'[7]

Finally, the Court should also consider whether inability might be triggered by a situation in which a State is unable to prosecute *effectively*, depending on the facts of the situation. Whenever conduct extends over several jurisdictions or the alleged crime is connected to several States, such as in a situation of joint criminal responsibility with suspects or indicted persons of different nationalities, difficulties and obstacles obtaining the accused or securing evidence are likely to arise. On the one hand, each State could be regarded as 'unable' to prosecute the crime or the crimes as a whole; on the other hand, it could be argued that the ICC as a single forum would avoid conflicts among different national jurisdictions and therefore qualify as the most 'convenient' forum. If the whole idea of complementarity relies on the assumption that as a matter of principle the national court is the one better placed to proceed,

> 'States should not underestimate the many difficulties involved in carrying out investigations and concluding a trial in situations in which (most of) the evidence is to be found in other States or when the suspect or accused is not on their territory. They should, therefore, carefully examine whether or not the Court might be in a better position to adjudicate, and refrain from acting themselves if this seems to be the case.'[8]

4.   THE ASSESSMENT OF COMPLEMENTARITY: THE NEED FOR DIALOGUE

The call for compliance can further be regarded as a corollary to the need to assess complementarity within the context of a dynamic process. Jann Kleffner refers to such a process as 'interaction',[9] I would rather refer to it as 'procedural dialogue'. Irrespective of personal preferences in terminology, the idea remains to a great extent the same.

---

[7]   Ibid. preamble para. 4.

[8]   A. Cassese, P. Gaeta and J. Jones (eds.), *The Rome Statute of the International Criminal Court: A Commentary* (Oxford, Oxford University Press 2002) 1906.

[9]   Kleffner 82.

There are several indicia in the constitutive instruments of the Court pointing to the fact that the assessment of complementarity is the outcome of an ongoing process. The main actors of this process are the Court, on the one side, and national jurisdictions, on the other side. To a certain extent, the Rules of Procedure and Evidence[10] and the Regulations of the Court[11] mandate a similar dialogue to happen within the Court itself among its various organs. Rule 107, paragraph 2, provides: 'The Pre-Trial Chamber may request the Prosecutor to transmit the information or documents in his or her possession, or summaries thereof, that the Chamber considers necessary for the conduct of the review.'[12] Pursuant to Article 53, paragraph 3(a), of the Rome Statute, the Pre-Trial Chamber may review the Prosecutor's decision not to initiate an investigation or not to prosecute.[13] Regulation 48 empowers the Pre-Trial Chamber to 'request the Prosecutor to provide specific or additional information or documents in his or her possession, or summaries thereof, that the Pre-Trial Chamber considers necessary in order to properly exercise its functions and responsibilities.'[14]

The procedural steps set forth in the Statute and the Rules as key elements for the correct functioning of the complementarity regime, with a view to allowing the Court to assume jurisdiction whenever appropriate, should be borne in mind in this context. Significant provisions in this respect are enshrined in some of the Rules. Rule 51 provides:

> 'In considering the matters referred to in article 17, paragraph 2, and in the context of the circumstances of the case, the Court may consider, *inter alia*, information that the State ... may choose to bring to the attention of the Court showing that its courts meet internationally recognized norms and standards for the independent and impartial prosecution of similar conduct, or that the State has confirmed in writing to the Prosecutor that the case is being investigated and prosecuted'.[15]

---

[10] Rules of Procedure and Evidence (Rules) ICC-ASP/1/3 (September 2002).
[11] Regulations of the Court (Regulations) ICC-BD/01-01-04 (adopted 26 May 2004).
[12] Rules (n. 10) Rule 107 para. 2.
[13] Rome Statute (n. 1) Art. 53 para. 3a.
[14] Regulations (n. 11) Regulation 48.
[15] Rules (n. 10) Rule 51.

Rule 52, paragraph 2, allows a State to 'request additional information from the Prosecutor to assist it in the application of article 18, paragraph 2',[16] that is in deciding whether to ask for the investigation to be deferred to its own jurisdiction after the Prosecutor has determined that there is a reasonable basis to initiate an investigation.

The ultimate aim of this dialogue consists of ensuring that the goals underlying the Statute are achieved. Here, again, we see the rules governing complementarity at work as 'catalysts for compliance'.

5. COMPLEMENTARITY AND THE 'SUPERVISORY' ROLE OF THE COURT

Jann Kleffner claims that, in carrying out the procedural dialogue provided under the Statute for the purpose of complementarity, the Court performs 'a supervisory function'.[17]

Here, I would like to strike a note of caution. On the one hand, the assumption sounds most reasonable and perfectly in line with the role that the ICC is called to play *vis-à-vis* the commission of the most heinous crimes. On the other hand, however, we should bear in mind that the idea of a 'supervising' court was explicitly rejected by drafters of the Statute. Therefore, it seems preferable to construe the role of the Court along the lines of a strictly objective assessment of the substantive requirements for complementarity and within the procedural framework in the Statute. The notion of 'unavailability', if construed under the terms proposed above, provides us with an appropriate tool to this effect.

6. COMPLEMENTARITY AND VIOLATIONS OF DUE PROCESS OCCURRING TO THE DETRIMENT OF THE ACCUSED

As a whole, the idea of complementarity triggering an 'affectionate partnership'[18] between the Court and national jurisdictions very much deserves

---

[16] Ibid. Rule 52 para. 2.
[17] Kleffner 82.
[18] Ibid.

to be pursued. What matters, ultimately, is that the object and purpose of the Statute (to end impunity for the perpetrators of the worst crimes) is achieved. In this respect, I would recommend caution in saying: 'The substance of complementarity would seem to provide only very limited room, if any, for the ICC to assume jurisdiction in cases where there have been violations of norms of due process, which work to the disadvantage of the person concerned.'[19]

This conclusion sounds defeating of the high purposes which presided over the very establishment of the ICC. Negotiations leading to the Statute constantly relied on a twofold understanding: On the one hand, the ICC would complement, as opposed to replace, national jurisdictions; otherwise stated, national courts would operate as a sort of 'first line of defence' against impunity and a sort of division of labour between the national courts and the ICC could be envisaged. On the other hand, however, it was never held that the ICC should play a residual or minor role. In other words, the balance between national and international jurisdiction should not be achieved to the detriment of the fundamental purpose of having in place an effective system of prevention and punishment of the crimes covered by the Statute.

That said, it is undoubtedly true and accurate to say that the Rome Statute, and more specifically Article 17, seems to have been drafted with the following in mind: first and foremost, the scenario of a conflict between a State claiming jurisdiction in a situation, on the one side, and the ICC also claiming jurisdiction in the same situation, on the other side. As Jann Kleffner puts it, 'the formal framework of complementarity encapsulates a relationship between national criminal jurisdictions and the ICC, which is to a large extent characterized by *antagonism*.'[20] However, the positive approach to complementarity advocated by the very idea of an 'affectionate partnership' or of complementarity as a 'catalyst for compliance', could and should allow us to go further.

Complementarity should be regarded not so much as a duty or as an imposed rule, but rather as an opportunity for both States and the Court to achieve goals which are common and ultimately pertain to the international community as a whole. It is true that Article 17, paragraph 2, requires the Court to look at 'the principles of due process recognized by international

---

[19] Ibid. n. 12.
[20] Ibid. 84.

law'[21] for the purpose of determining the unwillingness of a State to investigate and prosecute duly; that is, not in the usual perspective of protection
of the individual *against* possible abuses by the State, but rather under the
perspective of their possible violation to the benefit of the suspect, that is,
with a view to shielding him or her from punishment. However, the role of
the Court, as an international body complementing national jurisdictions in
meting out fair punishment for the most serious crimes, suggests that a
violation of due process occurring not to the benefit but *to the detriment* of
the person subjected to the proceedings would equally result in the State
being held unwilling and the case being admissible before the Court.

This view seems to be supported not only by the very objectives pursued
by creating the ICC but also by two major textual arguments: First, for the
purposes of complementarity, a departure from principles of due process is
to be ultimately assessed against the parameter of 'bringing the person to
justice'. This seems not only to evoke ascertainment of guilt and subsequent punishment, but rather, more broadly, to convey the need for an impartial assessment of the actual position and role of the accused. Second,
Article 54, paragraph 1(a), of the Statute requires the Prosecutor '[i]n order
to establish the truth, [to] extend the investigation to cover all facts and
evidence relevant to an assessment of whether there is criminal responsibility under this Statute and, in doing so, [to] investigate incriminating and
exonerating circumstances equally.'[22]

Moreover, in practical terms it would be extremely difficult for the Court
to determine *ex ante* whether a violation of the principles of due process
occurred to the detriment or to the benefit of the accused. Actually, this
narrow reading of the parameter of the internationally recognized principles
of due process, that is, as if they only include violations occurring to the
detriment of the accused, might ultimately result in increasing, as opposed
to diminishing, the discretion of the Court. This would run counter to the
widely shared assumption that reference to those principles was meant to

---

[21] Rome Statute (n. 1) Art. 17 para. 2.
[22] Ibid. Art. 54 para. 1a.

circumscribe the discretion of the Court when assessing the willingness of a State.[23]

---

[23] See chapter 4, 'The Admissibility Test before the International Criminal Court under Special Consideration of Amnesties and Truth Commissions', contains an opening in this respect. Art. 20, para. 3(b), of the Rome Statute (n. 1) provides an exception to the *ne bis in idem* rule and allows a retrial before the ICC when proceedings at the national level 'were not conducted independently or impartially in accordance with the norms of due process recognized by international law and were conducted in a manner which, in the circumstances, was inconsistent with an intent to bring the person concerned to justice.' This provision applies irrespective of whether the lack of independence or impartiality 'affect[ed] the concerned person positively or negatively.' Cárdenas Aravena 127.

Chapter 4
THE ADMISSIBILITY TEST BEFORE THE INTERNATIONAL CRIMINAL COURT UNDER SPECIAL CONSIDERATION OF AMNESTIES AND TRUTH COMMISSIONS

Claudia Cárdenas Aravena*

1. INTRODUCTION

With the entry into force of the Rome Statute,[1] a State's competence to try international crimes remains untouched. According to the complementarity principle, cases of genocide, crimes against humanity, war crimes and (upon definition) the crime of aggression are to be tried by States. The ICC only acts when States do not undertake proceedings or do not do it properly. In order to apply this complementarity principle, the Court has to undertake an admissibility exam[2] for each case before it.[3] This admissibility test de-

---

* LL.M., Ph.D. candidate, Humboldt University (Berlin). This paper is a synopsis of my doctoral research on the admissibility test. The full text of my doctoral thesis will be published at the beginning of 2005 under the title *Die Zulässigkeitsprüfung vor dem Internationalen Strafgerichtshof: Zur Auslegung des Artikels 17 IStGH-Statut (unter besonderer Berücksichtigung von Amnestien und Wahrheitskommissionen)*. I would sincerely like to thank Joseph Windsor, LL.M. candidate, for language corrections and various comments, as well as Boris Burghardt, Ph.D. candidate, and Professor Dr. Gerhard Werle for their useful observations and discussion of the article. All views expressed and errors are solely the responsibility of the author. The author can be contacted at cardenascl@yahoo.de.

[1] Rome Statute of the International Criminal Court (Rome Statute) (adopted 17 July 1998, entered into force 1 July 2002) UN Doc. A/CONF.183/9.

[2] Cf. ibid. Art. 53 para. 1c, Art. 53 para. 2c, Art. 19 para. 1. The close relationship between the complementarity principle and the admissibility test is explicitly recognized in Article 17, paragraph 1, of the Rome Statute with reference to para. 10 of the preamble and to Art. 1 of the Statute; cf. J.T. Holmes, 'The Complementarity Principle', in Lee (ed.), *The International Criminal Court: The Making of the Rome Statute* (The Hague, Kluwer 1999) 41, 42; M. Boot, *Genocide, Crimes Against Humanity, War Crimes* (Antwerp, Intersentia 2002) 48, 52; Human Rights Watch, *Justice in Balance* (New York, Human Rights Watch

J.K. Kleffner & G. Kor (eds.), Complementary Views on Complementarity
© 2006, T·M·C·ASSER PRESS, The Hague, The Netherlands and the Authors

termines to what extent the national judicial systems may be complemented by the ICC.

The admissibility test regulated by Article 17 of the ICC Statute is supposed to give the material framework for the discretionary powers of the Prosecutor. His powers to consider whether an investigation or a prosecution by the ICC serves the interests of justice in a given case apply only within admissible cases.[4] So, while an inadmissible case cannot be tried by the Court, the fact that a case is admissible before the ICC does not mean that the Court will necessarily have to try it.

In the following, the admissibility test in Article 17 is explained in section 2 and illustrated in section 3 by applying it in cases involving amnesties and truth commissions.

2.   THE ADMISSIBILITY TEST FOR THE ICC

According to Article 17 of the ICC Statute, as a starting-point, the admissibility of each case before the ICC is presumed. A case becomes inadmissible when a ground for inadmissibility is proven, unless one or more of its exceptions – regulated as a comprehensive *numerus clauses* – are also proven. In the last constellation, although a State has taken action regarding the case, its action was not enough to satisfy the expectations of the States Parties to the Statute so that the ICC may exercise its complementary jurisdiction.

1998) 70; R. Philips, 'The International Criminal Law Statute: Jurisdiction and Admissibility', 10 *Crim L Forum* (1999), 61, 63; G. Seidel and C. Stahn, 'Das Statut des Weltstrafgerichtshofs – Ein Überblick über Entstehung, Inhalt und Bedeutung', 21 *Jura* (1999),14, 16.

[3] Cf. F. Lattanzi, *The International Criminal Court: Comments on the Draft Statute* (Naples, Editoriale Scientifica 1998) 1, 10; ICC Office of the Prosecutor, 'Informal Expert Paper: The Principle of Complementarity' (Informal Expert Paper) (2003) 21 para. 68 <http://www.icc-cpi.int/library/organs/otp/complementarity.pdf> (20 July 2005); Boot (n. 2) 61; M. Vouilloz, *La Jurisdiction Pénale Internationale* (Basel, Helbing & Lichtenhahn 2001) 86; H. Olásolo, 'Issues Regarding the General Powers of the ICC Prosecutor under Art. 42 of the Rome Statute', 3 *Intl Crim L Rev* (2003), 87, 98 ff.

[4] Rome Statute (n. 1) Art. 53 paras. 1b, 1c, 2b, 2c.

2.1   Grounds for inadmissibility

According to the first paragraph of Article 17, a case is admissible before the ICC unless:

'(a) The case is being investigated or prosecuted by a State which has jurisdiction over it ...
(b) The case has been investigated by a State which has jurisdiction over it and the State has decided not to prosecute the person concerned ...
(c) The person concerned has already been tried for conduct which is the subject of the complaint, and the trial by the Court is not permitted under article 20 paragraph 3;
(d) The case is not of sufficient gravity to justify further action by the Court.'

In the following, the interpretation of each of these grounds for inadmissibility is considered.

2.1.1   *Current investigation or prosecution*

A case is to be left to the national prosecution systems, in the first place, when a State is currently investigating or prosecuting it. This ground for inadmissibility, stated in Article 17, paragraph 1(a), requires two elements: first 'investigation or prosecution' and second 'by a State which has jurisdiction over it'. An investigation is to be understood as a systematic inquiry about the facts of a crime and about participation in it. A prosecution is to be understood as the opening and undertaking of a judicial criminal process. The proceedings have to be undertaken by a State. That means that investigation or prosecution undertaken by other subjects of public international law, such as the United Nations, or by non-governmental organizations (NGOs) cannot be subsumed under this ground for inadmissibility.

Moreover, the acting State has to have jurisdiction over the case. In this regard, taking into account the internationally recognized principles upon which international criminal jurisdiction may be founded – in particular the principle of universal jurisdiction for crimes under international law – each and every State has jurisdiction over genocide, crimes against humanity and war crimes.[5] As a practical result, the expression 'a State which has

---

[5]   Cf. Amnesty International, *Universal Jurisdiction* (Legal Memorandum) (1 Septem-

jurisdiction over it' means any State[6] so that every national investigation or prosecution has to be considered.[7] This reference emerged when the juris-

---

ber 2001) AI-Index IOR 53/002/2001; H.P. Kaul and C. Kreß, 'Jurisdicción y Cooperación en el Estatuto de la Corte Penal Internacional: Principios y Compromisos', in K. Ambos (ed.), *La Nueva Justicia Penal Supranacional* (Valencia, Tirant lo Blanch 2002) 297, 302 ff.; M.C. Bassiouni, *Crimes against Humanity in International Law* (The Hague, Kluwer 1992) 504; M.C. Bassiouni, 'Universal Jurisdiction for International Crimes: Historical Perspectives and Contemporary Practice', 42 *Virginia J of Intl L* (2001), 81, 107 ff.; L. Benavides, 'The Universal Jurisdiction Principle: Nature and Scope', 19 *Anuario Mexicano de Derecho Internacional* (2001) 19; B. Broomhall, *International Justice and the International Criminal Court* (Oxford, Oxford University Press 2003) 110, 115; G. Conso, 'Some Reflections on the International Criminal Court', in F. Lattanzi and W. Schabas (eds.), *Essays on the Rome Statute of the International Criminal Court*, Vol. I (Alto, Il Sirente Ripa Fagnano 1999) 1; Preparatory Commmittee, 'The Jurisdiction of the International Criminal Court, an Informal Discussion Paper Submitted by Germany' (23 March 1998) UN Doc. A/AC.249/1998/DP.2; *Prosecutor v. Ntuyahaga* (Decision on the Prosecutor's Motion to Withdraw the Indictment) ICTR-98-40-T (18 March 1999); International Committee of the Red Cross *State Consent Regime v. Universal Jurisdiction* (10 December 1997) <http://www.icrc.org/web/eng/siteeng0.nsf/iwpList320/F4607C74CA18E5F5C1256B66005C27D5> (20 July 2005); M.T. Kamminga, 'Lessons Learned from the Exercise of Universal Jurisdiction in Respect of Gross Human Rights Offences', 23 *Human Rights Q* (2001), 940, 947; C. Kreß, 'Völkerstrafrecht und Weltrechtspflegeprinzip im Blickfeld des Internationalen Gerichtshofs. Zum Votenstreit der Richter des IGH im Haftbefehlsfall (Demokratische Republik Kongo gegen Belgien)', 114 *Zeitschrift für die Gesamte Strafrechtswissenschaft* (2002),818, 832 ff.; W. Schabas, *Introduction to the International Criminal Court* (The Hague, Kluwer 2001) 60; W. Schabas, 'La Cour Criminelle Internationale: un Pas de Plus contre l'Impunité', in *L'influence du Droit International sur la Pratique du Droit au Canada* (1999) 3, 6; M. Starita, 'Amnesty for Crimes Against Humanity: Coordinating the State and Individual Responsibility for Gross Violations of Human Rights', *Italian Ybk of Intl L* (1999), 86, 103; O. Triffterer, 'Legal and Political Implications of Domestic Ratification and Implementation Processes', in C. Kreß and F. Lattanzi (eds.), *The Rome Statute and Domestic Legal Orders* (Alto, Il Sirente Ripa di Fagnano 2000) 17 ff.; *Principles of International Co-operation in the Detention, Arrest, Extradition and Punishment of Persons Guilty of War Crimes and Crimes Against Humanity* para. 1 G.A. Res. 3074 (XXVIII) ; Vouilloz (n. 3) 86; A.L. Zuppi, *La Jurisdicción Extraterritorial y la Corte Penal Internacional* (Buenos Aires, Academia Nacional de Derecho y Ciencias Sociles 2001).

    [6] Cf. L. Condorelli, 'La Cour Pénale Internationale: Un Pas de Géant (Pourvu qu'il soit accompli...)', 103 *Revue Général de Droit International Public* (1999), 7, 20 fn. 26; Kamminga (n. 5) 951; C. Stahn, 'Zwischen Weltfrieden und Materieller Gerechtigkeit: Die Gerichtsbarkeit des Ständigen Internationalen Strafgerichtshofs', *Europäische Grundrechte-Zeitschrift* (1998) 577, 589; M.C. Escobar Hernández, 'El Principio de Complementariedad', in J.A. Yáñez-Barnuevo (ed.), *La Justicia Penal Internacional* (Madrid, Casa de América 2001) 78, 83.
    [7] Cf. Boot (n. 2) 52.

diction *ratione materiae* of the ICC included treaty crimes, for which not every State is competent. They were confronted with the core crimes of the ICC Statute and with the treaty crimes as 'crimes in respect of which universal jurisdiction already existed'.[8]

2.1.2 *Past investigation and decision not to prosecute*

To fulfil the requirements of this second ground for inadmissibility, a State must have undertaken a systematic inquiry into the facts of an international crime within the jurisdiction of the ICC and into the participation in it. Further, the same State must have decided not to prosecute the case.

2.1.3 *Ne bis in idem principle*

In the third place, a case is inadmissible before the ICC if it has been decided with *res judicata* effect. There is a reference to Article 20, paragraph 3, of the ICC Statute, which regulates the *ne bis in idem* principle.

2.1.4 *Insufficient gravity of the case*

The insufficient gravity of a given case is an objective criterion. It is based on the case itself and not on the existence or nature of a national action concerning it. This is why this ground for inadmissibility does not have any exceptions. For the same reason, one must reject the opinion that the mere fact that cases are being or have been investigated by a truth commission makes them fall under the ground for inadmissibility in Article 17, paragraph 1(d), as a consequence of the fact that truth commissions would partially fulfil the goals of criminal prosecution.[9]

The proof of this standard should be made at the outset, even though it is regulated as the fourth criterion, because this proof has to be made in each and every case. Whether a case is being or has been investigated, as well as the other grounds for inadmissibility, is only relevant where the case is

---

[8] Cf. Preparatory Commmittee, 'Proceedings of the Preparatory Committee during March-April and August 1996', Vol. I (1996) 26.

[9] Cf. J. Meißner, *Die Zusammenarbeit mit dem Internationalen Strafgerichtshof nach dem Römischen Statut* (Munich, Beck 2003) 80 ff.

indeed grave enough. The other three grounds for inadmissibility, on the contrary, will not be proven cumulatively because they cannot coexist.

The establishment of an international criminal court is justified by international concern about the cases within its jurisdiction. The elements which give rise to this international concern are expressed in the chapeaux of Articles 6 and 7 for genocide and crimes against humanity and in paragraph 1 of Article 8 for war crimes, as well as in the element of the war situation in the commission of the crime. The same individual conduct constituting crimes under international law, such as murder and bodily harm, do not require these elements under national law. Therefore, in this case they do not fall within the ICC's jurisdiction, no matter how grave the conduct is in other respects. Because these elements turn national crimes into 'the most serious crimes of concern to the international community as a whole',[10] one can assume that they are the key to an objective determination of the gravity of the crime relevant to the ICC Statute. The 'sufficient gravity' required for the admissibility of the case according to Article 17, paragraph 1(d), is then to be understood as an intensification of the gravity required by conduct to be considered an international crime. The conclusion is then that, if these elements are not the principal factor in the crime, the case is not of sufficient gravity from the point of view of the ICC.[11] The application of this ground for inadmissibility will be rather exceptional, taking into account the inherent gravity of the core crimes of the ICC Statute. In the case of genocide, its occurrence is even excluded because the intent to destroy, the definitive element of genocide, is required for the existence of the crime to be determined.

2.2   Exceptions to the grounds of inadmissibility

The Statute provides for exceptions to the first three grounds for inadmissibility. Under Article 17, paragraph 1(a) and (b), the case is admissible before the ICC when the State is unwilling or unable genuinely to carry out the investigation or prosecution.[12] For Article 17, paragraph 1(c), the exceptions are regulated by Article 20, paragraph 3(c).

---

[10]   Rome Statute (n. 1) preamble para. 4, Art. 1, Art. 5 para. 1.

[11]   Cf. *Ybk of the Intl L Commission* (1994) 2356th meeting 193 para. 73.

[12]   Rome Statute (n. 1) Art. 17 paras. 2 and 3.

2.2.1 *The State is unwilling or unable genuinely to investigate or prosecute*

Paragraphs 1(a) and (b) of Article 17 have the same exceptions: A case actually under investigation or prosecution is inadmissible 'unless the State is unwilling or unable genuinely to carry out an investigation or prosecution.'[13] A case, which has been investigated and in respect of which the State has decided not to prosecute, is inadmissible 'unless the decision resulted from the unwillingness or inability of the State genuinely to prosecute.'[14] The adverb 'genuinely' emphasizes that a mock proceeding will not satisfy the requirements of this exception and that the case would then become admissible.[15]

Both concepts – 'unwilling' and 'unable' – are often confused and treated simply as one and the same although they are regulated separately as alternatives, or they are considered as a synonym for the admissibility test[16] although they are only one part of it. Paragraphs 2 and 3 of Article 17 contain exhaustive legal definitions of both terms, adopted as those best reflecting the complementary function of the ICC and – as usual with the ICC Statute – as those on which a general consensus finally was reached.[17]

---

[13] Ibid. Art. 17 para. 1(a).

[14] Ibid. Art. 17 para. 1(b).

[15] Cf. Informal Expert Paper (n. 3) 8 para. 22; Holmes (n. 2) 49 ff.; J.T. Holmes, 'Complementarity: National Courts versus the ICC', in A. Cassese, P. Gaeta, J. Jones (eds.), *The Rome Statute of the International Criminal Court* (Oxford, Oxford University Press 2002) 667, 674; P. Kirsch and D. Robinson, 'Reaching Agreement at the Rome Conference', in A. Cassese, P. Gaeta, J. Jones (eds.), *The Rome Statute of the International Criminal Court* (Oxford, Oxford University Press 2002) 67, 82; L.N. Sadat Wexler, 'Observations on the Consolidated ICC Text before the Final Session of the Preparatory Committee', 13 bis *Nouvelles Ètudes Pénales* (1998), 17, 24; W. Schabas, *An Introduction to the International Criminal Court* (Cambridge, Cambridge University Press 2001) 67.

[16] Cf. ICC Press Release, 'Communications Received by the Office of the Prosecutor of the ICC' (16 July 2003) No. pids.009.2003-EN p 2 < http://www.icc-cpi.int/library/press/mediaalert/16_july__english.pdf> (25 July 2005); ICC Office of the Prosecutor, 'Paper on Some Policy Issues before the Office of the Prosecutor' (2003) p 4 <http://www.icc-cpi.int/library/organs/otp/030905_Policy_Paper.pdf> (20 July 2005).

[17] Cf. prior expressions in *Ybk of the Intl L Commission* (1994), Vol. II part 2 27.

2.2.1.1   Unwillingness to investigate or prosecute

The unwillingness of States genuinely to carry out an investigation or prosecution was accepted as an admissibility criterion before the ICC, despite concerns about State sovereignty, because otherwise a mock trial in a given State would be enough to prevent the ICC from exercising its jurisdiction.[18] According to Article 17, paragraph 2, it is understood that a State is unwilling genuinely to carry out the investigation or prosecution, when:

> '(a) The proceedings were or are being undertaken or the national decision was made for the purpose of shielding the person concerned from criminal responsibility for crimes within the jurisdiction of the Court referred to in article 5;
> (b) There has been an unjustified delay in the proceedings which in the circumstances is inconsistent with an intent to bring the person concerned to justice;
> (c) The proceedings were not or are not being conducted independently or impartially, and they were or are being conducted in a manner which, in the circumstances, is inconsistent with an intent to bring the person concerned to justice.'[19]

In the 1997 draft of the Preparatory Committee, a footnote indicates that in this article the term 'proceedings' refers to both investigations and prosecutions.[20] In the following, the different manifestations of unwillingness are briefly explained.

2.2.1.1.1   Shielding from criminal responsibility
Shielding a suspect or an accused from individual criminal responsibility is the prime example of a State's unwillingness genuinely to prosecute a case. It has even been expressed that this manifestation of unwillingness would include the other two scenarios listed in Article 17, paragraph 2.[21] The pur-

---

[18] Cf. Holmes (n. 2) 50.

[19] Rome Statute (n. 1) Art. 17 para. 2a-c.

[20] UN General Assembly Preparatory Committee on the Establishment of an International Criminal Court, 'Decisions Taken by the Preparatory Committee at Its Session Held from 4 to 15 August 1997' (14 August 1997) 11 fn. 24 UN Doc A/AC.249/1997/L.8/Rev.1.

[21] Cf. Holmes (n. 15) 675.

pose of shielding a person from criminal responsibility has to be manifest in the current investigation or prosecution[22] or be the motive for the decision not to prosecute.[23] The exception also applies when action is taken despite the certain, foreseeable result that the given person will be protected from criminal responsibility. The intention of a State as a whole must be contemplated, not just that of the implementing organ.[24]

2.2.1.1.2 Unjustified delay inconsistent with an intent to bring the person concerned to justice

This exception to inadmissibility requires a delay in the proceedings, such as when they have taken longer than other similar proceedings in the State concerned.[25] In proceedings without an available basis of comparison at the national level, for example, investigations by State-run truth commissions, there has to be an international comparison. Secondly, it requires that the delay is unjustified, meaning that the delay is avoidable but that State agents do not act with the obligatory due diligence. The third and final requirement is that the delay must be inconsistent with the intent to bring the person to justice. The delay then has to be such that a genuine State interest in holding the person concerned accountable for his or her deeds under due process of law is no longer plausible.[26] In order to determine when such an extent is reached, the particularities of each case have to be taken into account. The circumstances of the national judicial system and of the suspected person, the type of evidence, and the kind of proceedings undertaken should be decisive factors in the determination of an acceptable length of delay.

2.2.1.1.3 Lack of independence or impartiality inconsistent with an intent to bring the person concerned to justice

Proceedings are impartial when they are not biased. They are independent when the entity in charge of the decision is not subjected to improper influ-

---

[22] Rome Statute (n. 1) Art. 17 para. 1a.

[23] Ibid. Art. 17 para. 1b.

[24] Cf. Meißner (n. 9) 83 ff.; Informal Expert Paper (n. 3) 14 para. 45.

[25] Cf. Holmes (n. 15) 676; A. Zimmermann, 'Die Schaffung eines Ständigen Internationalen Strafgerichtshofes', 58 *Zeitschrift für Ausländisches Öffentliches Recht und Völkerrecht* (1998), 47, 98 ff.

[26] Cf. Zimmermann (n. 25) 98.

ence. When proceedings are impartial and independent, the decision-making is based exclusively on the merits of the proceeding. This exception requires the lack of one of these two elements in the national proceedings. Moreover, proceedings have to be conducted in a manner that is incompatible with an intent to bring the person concerned to justice, that is to subject him or her to due process of law and, where required, to punish him or her. In criminal processes, this last requirement is automatically fulfilled by a lack of independence or impartiality as judicial independence and impartiality are necessary elements of due process.

2.2.1.2   Inability to investigate or prosecute

Under the 'unwillingness test' the State's *bona fides* receive the most attention. Under the 'inability test' of Article 17, paragraph 3, the situation is not the same. Here, a State may be willing to investigate or prosecute, but it cannot. As a result of a total or substantial collapse or unavailability of its national judicial system, the State is simply unable genuinely to carry out the proceedings.

2.2.1.2.1   Unavailability of a national judicial system
The judicial system is unavailable when it is non-existent.[27] This is the only interpretation of the norm compatible with the authentic Spanish text of the Statute.[28] Article 33 of the Vienna Convention on the Law of Treaties presumes that, when a treaty has been authenticated in two or more languages, as the ICC Statute has been pursuant to Article 128, each authentic text has the same meaning and is equally legally binding.[29] Therefore, when a judicial system is unavailable according to Article 17, paragraph 3, investigations but not prosecutions would be possible.

---

[27] Contrast Meißner (n. 9) 87; Informal Expert Paper (n. 3) 15 para. 50, repeated in Annex 4 31.

[28] The Spanish text of the Rome Statute (n. 1) Art. 17 para. 3 reads: 'A fin de determinar la incapacidad para investigar o enjuiciar en un asunto determinado, la Corte determinará si el Estado, debido al colapso total o sustancial de su administración nacional de justicia o al hecho de que *carece* de ella, no puede …' (emphasis added).

[29] Vienna Convention on the Law of Treaties (VCLT) Art. 33 paras. 1 and 2 (adopted on 22 May 1969, entered into force 27 January 1980), 1155 *UNTS* 331.

2.2.1.2.2   Total or substantial collapse of a national judicial system

A State is unable genuinely to prosecute when its justice system is at least substantially collapsed. This is the case when its deficiencies are irremediable and, as a whole, it does not function as a system anymore. The system fails when its basic tasks – investigating facts of the crime and the persons involved, proving the charges and, if a culprit is found, punishing him or her – cannot be fulfilled. The State could be referred to as a 'failed State'[30] in this respect. If the collapse is merely temporary or its effects only reach a part of the territory of the State, the requirements for this exception are not fulfilled and the case is inadmissible before the ICC.[31] As examples of the effects of a relevant collapse, the Statute mentions the inability to obtain the accused or the necessary evidence and testimony.

These are the basic definitions of unwillingness and inability according to the ICC Statute.

2.2.2   *Exceptions to the ne bis in idem principle*

As exceptions to the third ground for inadmissibility before the ICC, the *ne bis in idem* principle contained in Article 20, paragraph 3, one finds two cases of the so-called 'sham exception', according to which mock trials should not be an impediment to new proceedings.[32] These two exceptions were primarily taken from Article 17, paragraph 2.[33] A case is admissible before the ICC, although it has already been tried, if the proceedings in the national court:

---

[30] Cf. Seidel and Stahn (n. 2) 16; C. Tomuschat, 'The Duty to Prosecute International Crimes Committed by Individuals', in Cremer and others (eds.), *Tradition und Weltoffenheit des Rechts – Festschrift für Helmut Steinberger* (Berlin, Springer 2002) 215, 340; Zimmermann (n. 25) 97 ff.

[31] Cf. Holmes (n. 15) 677.

[32] Cf. B. Berg, 'The 1994 I.L.C. Draft Statute for an International Criminal Court: A Principled Appraisal of Jurisdictional Structure', 28 *Case Western Reserve J of Intl L* (1996) 221, 247.

[33] Cf. L.N. Sadat, *The International Criminal Court and the Transformation of International Law: Justice for the New Millenium* (New York, Transnational Publishers 2002) 190; I. Tallgren, 'Article 20', in Triffterer (ed.), *Commentary on the Rome Statute of the International Criminal Court* (Baden-Baden, Nomos 1999) 419, 430.

'(a) Were for the purpose of shielding the person concerned from criminal responsibility for crimes within the jurisdiction of the Court, or

(b) Otherwise were not conducted independently or impartially in accordance with the norms of due process recognized by international law and were conducted in a manner which, in the circumstances, was inconsistent with an intent to bring the person concerned to justice.'[34]

2.2.2.1 Purpose of shielding

Here, the analysis is largely the same as in the above discussion of Article 17, paragraph 2(a). However, the gravity of the sentence is a specific criterion to be considered when determining whether shielding should serve as an exception to the *ne bis in idem* principle.[35] This does not mean that each acquittal or mild penalty for an individual accused of committing international crimes is to be interpreted as an indicator of the purpose of shielding. The presumption of innocence applies in international criminal law as well. The decisive issue is whether the decision was made based on the merits of the case or whether political aims to shield the person played a role.[36] The decision regarding the penalty given an accused convicted of specific criminal conduct is usually an internal affair, but this national decision cannot be respected if it is misused to shield a person from criminal liability according to international law. If the criminal proceeding is misused to protect the person concerned, it has the purpose of shielding and the case is admissible before the ICC despite any national judgment.

2.2.2.2 Lack of independence or impartiality inconsistent with an intent to bring the person concerned to justice

As for this exception, the analysis parallels that for Article 17, paragraph 2(c), above. However, in Article 20, paragraph 3(b), the norms of due process recognized by international law are the chosen criteria. Therefore, inconsistency with the intent to bring the person concerned to justice has to be necessarily inferred from any lack of independence or impartiality as

---

[34] Rome Statute (n. 1) Art. 20 para. 3a-b.

[35] Cf. Tallgren (n. 33) 430-31; Zimmermann (n. 25) 47.

[36] Cf. Informal Expert Paper (n. 3) 14 para. 46 (under 'unwillingness').

both elements are basic requirements of due process. The main difference from the first exception is that the lack of independence or impartiality can affect the concerned person positively or negatively.[37]

3.   AMNESTIES AND TRUTH COMMISSIONS IN RELATION TO THE ADMISSIBILITY TEST FOR THE ICC

Although experience has shown the importance of amnesties and truth commissions as tools of transitional justice in the last decades, neither of them is specifically regulated in the ICC Statute.[38] Therefore, a general regulation has to be applied. The few scholars who have discussed these issues do not generally identify the concrete norms that apply. In this context, it becomes necessary to analyse the topic in depth, on the basis of the Statute's regulation, in order to identify guidelines for the application of Article 17 of the ICC Statute.

3.1   **Amnesties**

Many questions arise in a discussion of amnesties and the ICC; however, the relevant questions for the present discussion are the following: Do they fall under the actual grounds for inadmissibility? If so, do they fulfil the

---

[37] Cf. Comisión Andina de Juristas, *La Corte Penal Internacional y los Países Andinos* (Lima, Comisión Andina de Juristas 2001) 149.

[38] Cf. M. Arsanjani, 'The International Criminal Court and National Amnesty Laws', *American Society of International Law Proceedings* (1997), 65, 67; J. Dugard, 'Dealing with Crimes of a Past Regime: Is Amnesty Still an Option?', 12 *Leiden J of Intl L* (1999), 1001, 1015; ELSA, *Handbook on the International Criminal Law* (Brussels, European Law Students' Association 1997) 81; ELSA, *Handbook on the International Criminal Law*, 2nd edn. (Brussels, European Law Students' Association 1998) 51; Human Rights Watch (n. 2) 72; Holmes (n. 2) 52; PrepCom Report 1996, Vol I para. 160; UN Commission on Human Rights, 'Report of the Special Rapporteur, Mr. Nigel S. Rodley, submitted pursuant to Commission on Human Rights Resolution 1997/38', (1997) para. 220 UN Doc. E/CN.4/1998/38; C. Van den Wyngaert and T. Ongena, '*Ne bis in idem* Principle, Including the Issue of Amnesty', in A. Cassese, P. Gaeta, J. Jones (eds.), *The Rome Statute of the International Criminal Court* (Oxford, Oxford University Press 2002) 705, 728; D. Robinson, 'Serving the Interests of Justice: Amnesties, Truth Commissions and the International Criminal Court', 14 *Eur J of Intl L* (2003), 481, 499; Schabas (n. 15) 69.

standards of the exceptions to the grounds for inadmissibility so that the given case would nonetheless be admissible? There is no simple and universally valid answer;[39] rather, amnesties must be categorized according to the criteria of the admissibility test, the various grounds for inadmissibility and their exceptions.

3.1.1 *Insufficiently grave cases*

In the first place, amnestied cases that are of insufficient gravity have to be differentiated because they will, in any event, be inadmissible before the ICC, according to Article 17, paragraph 1(d), of the ICC Statute.

3.1.2 *Sufficiently grave cases*

For the cases of sufficient gravity, one must further distinguish between de facto and de jure amnesties.

3.1.2.1 *De facto* amnesties

The first group, the *de facto* amnesties, merely describes the failure of the criminal justice system of a State even to investigate a crime. However, investigations by a truth commission could take place without being considered to effect a *de facto* amnesty because truth commissions do not directly seek punishment of the culprit. If there are no investigations at all, the case is admissible before the ICC because no ground for inadmissibility is fulfilled. If the concerned case is currently being investigated by a truth commission, it is inadmissible pursuant to Article 17, paragraph 1, of the ICC Statute. If the truth commission's investigation ends and no criminal proceeding follows, the case becomes admissible before the ICC as no ground for inadmissibility is fulfilled.

---

[39] Contrast Boot (n. 2) 54 ff.; Kamminga (n. 5) 957; C. Möller, *Völkerstrafrecht und Internationaler Strafgerichtshof* (Münster, Lit 2003) 614 ff.; A. O'Shea, *Amnesty for Crime in International Law and Practice* (The Hague, Kluwer 2002) 125; Escobar Hernández (n. 6) 97 ff.

3.1.2.2   *De jure* amnesties

In the following section, the attention will be on *de jure* amnesties, which are understood as the legal determination of the requirements for release from punishment, prosecution or even investigation for an indeterminate number of cases. Depending on the relevant norms and their interpretation, *de jure* amnesties can impede the investigation, the accusation, or the punishment in a given case.

3.1.2.2.1   As an impediment to investigation

If an amnesty law impedes an investigation by the criminal justice system, its effect is the same as that of a *de facto* amnesty. Thus, a case falling under the amnesty law is admissible before the ICC, provided that it is of sufficient gravity, because none of the grounds for inadmissibility are fulfilled. The only exception would be an investigation by a truth commission with the above described result of the admissibility test. Truth commissions dealing with a case covered by an amnesty are not forbidden by amnesty law because their proceedings do not foresee the punishment of those responsible, whereas the main goal of amnesties is to avoid punishment.

3.1.2.2.2   As an impediment to prosecution

When considering whether an amnesty has the effect of impeding a prosecution, the grounds for inadmissibility under Article 17, paragraph 1(a) and (b), are to be examined because Article 17, paragraph 1(c), presupposes a judicial sentence, which is impossible with this kind of amnesty and because Article 17, paragraph (d) will have already been examined.

Current investigation
If a State is currently investigating a case, the ground for inadmissibility under Article 17, paragraph 1(a), is fulfilled. Investigations could be directed by truth commissions or by prosecution agents in a criminal procedure (prosecutor or investigating judge). The question now is whether the requirements of unwillingness or inability according to the ICC Statute are also fulfilled. As the State is free to adopt or derogate from an amnesty law, one cannot speak of inability to prosecute, and neither of the manifestations

of unwillingness listed in Article 17, paragraph 2, can be *a priori* affirmed pending the investigative proceedings. The case would therefore likely be inadmissible although a case-by-case analysis is needed.

Past investigation and decision not to prosecute
The other applicable provision regarding this kind of amnesty is Article 17, paragraph 1(b). It applies when the case has been investigated and the decision not to prosecute has been made. Again, before affirming that a case is inadmissible, the exceptions to the grounds for inadmissibility must be examined. The application of an amnesty law is a clear example of a State deciding not to prosecute because it is unwilling to do so. This expression of unwillingness falls under Article 17, paragraph 2(a), of the ICC Statute; that is, the decision has been made in order to shield the given person from criminal responsibility.

The view has been expressed that to fulfil this exception, the shielding should be aimed at a specific person (the ICC Statute speaks about 'the person concerned'), which is not the case with an amnesty law that concerns an indeterminate number of persons.[40] To refute this argument, it has to be clarified that amnesty laws are enacted to release persons from criminal liability; that is, they have an inherent and immediate purpose of shielding, whether or not they pursue other goals that can always be claimed (even with blanket-self-amnesties) but are very difficult to prove. Acts of parliament, by their nature, apply to an indeterminate number of persons, while criminal procedures, by their nature, relate to individuals. In criminal procedures in which an amnesty law is applied, a decision is made that will shield only determinate individuals from criminal liability. The decision is made to apply the law and to fulfil its aims of shielding the person concerned from criminal liability. This situation falls under Article 17, paragraph 2(a) of the ICC Statute; therefore, the case is admissible before the ICC.

---

[40] Cf. F. Hoffmeister and S. Knoke, 'Das Vorermittlungsverfahren vor dem Internationalen Strafgerichtshof – Prüfstein für die Effektivität der neuen Gerichtsbarkeit im Völkerstrafrecht', 59 *Zeitschrift für Ausländisches Öffentliches Recht und Völkerrecht* (1999) 785, 799; A. Bruer-Schäfer, *Der Internationale Strafgerichtshof* (Frankfurt am Main, Lang 2001) 350.

3.1.2.2.3   As an impediment to punishment

The same arguments can be made in cases where a trial has taken place and a judgment has been passed but the perpetrator is then exempted from punishment. Although the requirements for inadmissibility in Article 17, paragraph 1(c), are fulfilled, the *ne bis in idem* principle is inapplicable because the exception in Article 20, paragraph 3(a), applies. In the national proceedings a law was applied, the immediate purpose of which was to avoid the consequences according to international criminal law in the case of conviction.[41] Thus, the proceedings in the other court were for the purpose of shielding the person concerned from criminal liability. Even if it were assumed that the main goal of granting amnesties is actually to further reconciliation, impunity is nonetheless a kind of 'collateral damage' certain to occur so that it must be considered part of the purpose.

Therefore, according to the ICC Statute and despite specific regulations, it can be concluded that decisions based on amnesties constitute grounds for admissibility before the ICC.[42] This conclusion is concordant with other international norms[43] and with the preamble to the ICC Statute,[44] which is part of its text and, as a consequence, as binding as the rest of the text.[45] Amnesties derogate from criminal law.[46] This fact combined with the general principle stating that national law may not derogate from international

---

[41] Contrast J. Gavron, 'Amnesties in the Light of Developments in International Law and the Establishment of the International Criminal Court', 51 *Intl and Comparative L Q* (2002), 91, 109 ff.

[42] For the view that the ICC remains nonetheless ambiguous on this matter, compare M. Scharf, 'Justice Versus Peace', in S. Sewall and C. Kaysen (eds.), *The United States and the International Criminal Court* (Lanham, Rowman & Littlefield 2000) 179, 186.

[43] Compare Gavron (n. 41) 94 ff. and repeated decisions of the Inter-American Commission on Human Rights since the 1990s: Reports No. 29/92 (1992-1993) paras. 37, 53; No. 34/96 (1996) paras. 105, 107; No. 36/96 (1996) paras. 61, 73, 86; No. 25/98 (1998) paras. 45, 50, 53.

[44] Cf. Rome Statute (n. 1) preamble paras. 4, 5, 6 and 10.

[45] See VCLT (n. 29) Art. 31 paras. 1 and 2.

[46] Cf. J.G. Schätzler, *Handbuch des Gnadenrechts* (Munich, Beck 1992) 208.

norms[47] confirms that national amnesty laws for international crimes are at least not applicable to other subjects of international law.[48]

3.2 Truth commissions

The concept of truth commissions yields very dissimilar phenomena, as can be seen in the cases of the commissions in Chile,[49] South Africa[50] and El Salvador.[51] What they all have in common is their nature as non-judicial

---

[47] Regarding the law of treaties, see VCLT (n. 29) Art. 27. Compare W. Burke-White, 'Reframing Impunity: Applying Liberal International Law Theory to an Analysis of Amnesty Legislation', 42 *Harvard Intl L J* (2001). 467, 478; B. Chigara, *Amnesty in International Law* (Cambridge, Harvard Law School 2002) 78; and F.A. Hammel, *Innerstaatliche Amnestien* (Frankfurt am Main, Lang 1993) 23-24, 124.

[48] Cf. Amnesty International, *Making the Right Choices I* (January 1997) AI-Index IOR 40/01/97 66; Amnesty International, *Making the Right Choices V* (May 1998) AI-Index IOR 40/10/98 34 ff.; Gavron (n. 41) 115; Kamminga (n. 5) 958; O'Shea (n. 39) 132; G. Werle, 'Rückwirkungsverbot und Staatskriminalität', 41 *Neue Juristische Wochenschrift* (2001), 3001, 3002. Compare also *Prosecutor* v. *Kallon and Kamara* (Decision on Challenge to Jurisdiction: Lomé Accord Amnesty) SCSL-04-15-PT-060-I, SCSL-04-15-PT-060-II (13 March 2004).

[49] *Comisión Nacional de Verdad y Reconciliación* instituted by Decreto Supremo N 355, Santiago, 25 April 1990. Compare, e.g., G. Klumpp, *Vergangenheitsbewältigung durch Wahrheitskommissionen – das Beispiel Chile* (Berlin, Berlin Verlag 2001).

[50] Cf. section 2 of the *Promotion of National Unity and Reconciliation Act* of 1995 cap. 2, 3 (1)(b); <http://www.doj.gov.za/trc/amntrans/index.htm> (20 July 2005); N. Durczac, *Der Versuch einer Vergangenheitsbewältigung in Südafrika durch die Wahrheits- und Versöhnungskommission* (Frankfurt am Main, Lang 2001); R. Goldstone, 'Justice as a Tool for Peace-Making: Truth Commissions and International Criminal Tribunals', 28 *New York U J of Intl L and Politics* (1996), 485, 493; P.K. Rakate, 'Towards a Restorative Model of Justice – The South African Experience', in J. Hasse, E. Müller and P. Schneider (eds.), *Humanitäres Völkerrecht* (Baden-Baden, Nomos 2001) 542, 542 ff.; critical E.H. McCarthy in R.L. Brooks (ed.), *When Sorry Isn't Enough* (New York, New York University Press 1999) 487, 487 ff.

[51] This commission was envisaged in the 'Mexico Agreements' from 27 April 1991. Compare T. Buergenthal, 'La Comisión de la Verdad para El Salvador', in T. Buergenthal and others (eds.), *Estudios Especializados de Derechos Humanos I* (San José, Instituto Internamericano de Derechos Humanos 1996) 11, 11 ff.; T. Buergenthal, 'The United Nations Truth Commission in El Salvador', in N.J. Kritz (ed.), *Transitional Justice* (Washington DC, United States Institute of Peace Press 1995) 292 ff.; and D.W. Cassel, 'International Truth Commissions and Justice', in N.J. Kritz (ed.), *Transitional Justice* (Washington DC, United States Institute of Peace Press 1995) 326 ff.

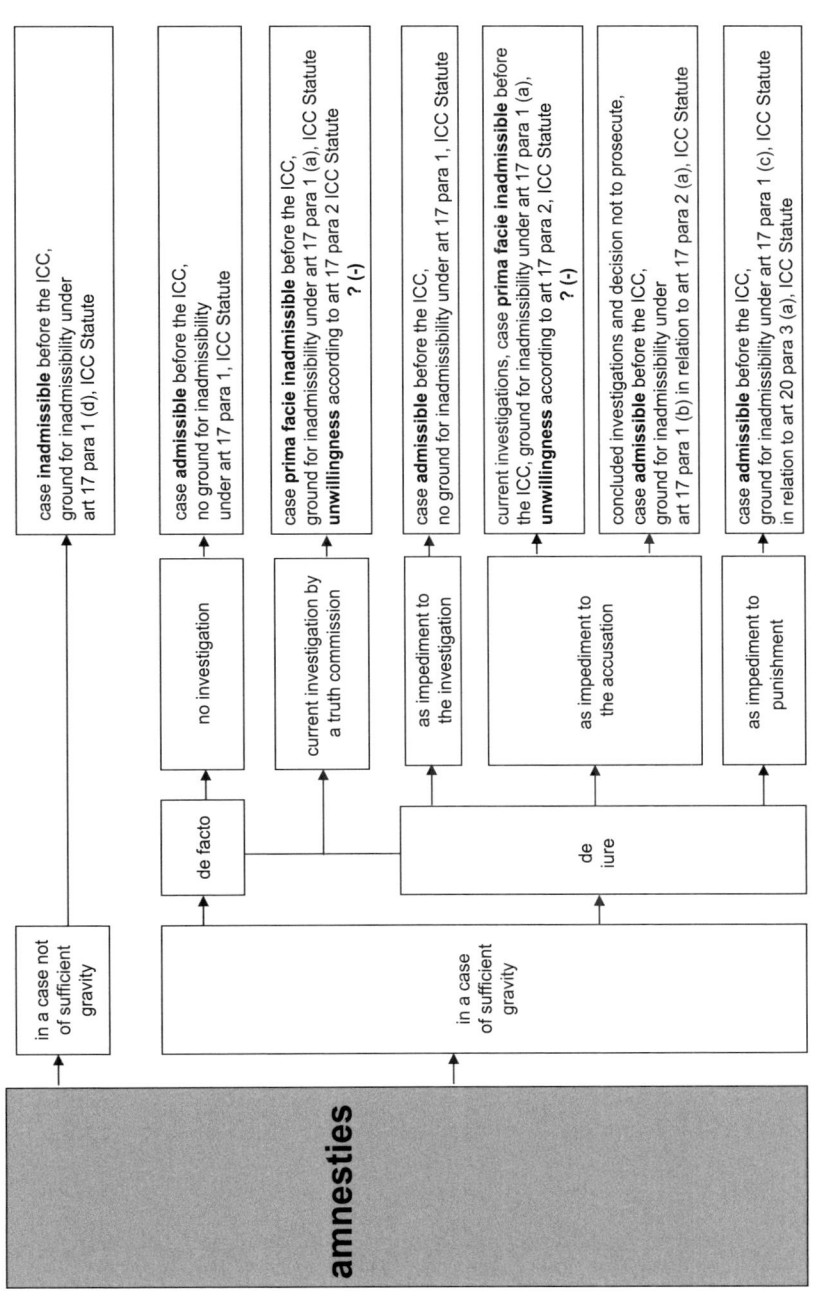

institutions that have the mission to reconstruct the history of a certain period to facilitate reconciliation in a given society.[52]

3.2.1   Insufficiently grave cases

In the first place, the cases that are investigated by truth commissions but
do not have sufficient gravity to be tried by the ICC have to be distinguished because these cases will never be admissible before the ICC, according to Article 17, paragraph 1(d), of the ICC Statute.

3.2.2   Sufficiently grave cases

For the cases of sufficient gravity, one must distinguish between non-State
run and State-run commissions.

3.2.2.1   Non-State-run organ

If a truth commission is not State-run, the case will be admissible before the
Court if it is of sufficient gravity and it is not or has not been genuinely
investigated or prosecuted by the State. None of the grounds for inadmissibility in Article 17, paragraph 1, of the ICC Statute will be satisfied.

3.2.2.2   State-run organ

If the truth commission is a State-run organ, further analysis is required. Its
mandate can be limited to reconstructing the historical events of the past or,
in addition, it may have the competence to grant amnesty.

3.2.2.2.1   Only historical record
In the case of truth commissions that seek only to clarify the past, the ground
for inadmissibility in Article 17, paragraphs 1(a) and 1(b), of the ICC Statute should be considered. Paragraph 1(c) of that article deals with cases
where a final judicial decision has been made, which does not apply here,

---

[52] Cf. C. Tomuschat, 'Clarification Commission in Guatemala', 23 *Human Rights Q*
(2001), 233, 235; P. Hayner, *Unspeakable Truths* (New York, Routledge 2001).

and paragraph 1(d) has been treated above. It follows that a distinction between investigations in progress and closed investigations must be drawn.

Current investigations
To determine the admissibility of a given case falling within the mandate of
a functioning State-run truth commission, one should consider whether the
truth commission is currently fulfilling its mandate. If so, and if the given
case falls within this mandate, it is to be considered as being currently investigated. Thus the requirements for the ground for inadmissibility in Article 17, paragraph 1(a), are fulfilled. It is then necessary to determine whether
the requirements of any of the exceptions in paragraphs 2 and 3 of Article
17 are satisfied.

Concerning the exception of unwillingness of the State, each of the three
alternatives can be neither affirmed nor negated *a priori* in the case of truth
commissions. Regarding Article 17, paragraph 2(c), of the ICC Statute (lack
of independence or impartiality inconsistent with intent to bring the person
concerned to justice), no judicial standards will be imposed because a truth
commission is not a court. Nevertheless, similar standards are required:
The personnel have to be unbiased and must act without improper influence.

The inability of a State genuinely to carry out an investigation or prosecution is specifically linked to criminal prosecutions in the Rome Statute.
Collapse and unavailability of the national judicial system are the only criteria provided to determine a State's ability genuinely to undertake proceedings. The basic aim here is that a State should only be able to forego the
complementary jurisdiction of the ICC if it can actually ultimately fulfil its
duty to punish the perpetrators of international crimes. Therefore, the Rome
Statute requires the determination of whether the judiciary functions as such,
so that the State has voluntarily taken the option of a truth commission,
probably as a first step in dealing with the past. If so, and no unwillingness
of the State can be proven, the case is inadmissible. If, on the contrary,
Article 17, paragraph 3, of the ICC Statute applies or unwillingness can be
proven, the case is admissible before the Court.

Concluded investigations
In the case of concluded investigations by a truth commission, a State sel-
dom makes the formal decision not to prosecute. Often a *de facto* amnesty

takes place, that is a mere omission by national judicial authorities once the investigations have been finished. If so, the case is admissible before the ICC, provided it is of sufficient gravity, because no ground for inadmissibility is fulfilled.

In cases where, on the contrary, a formal decision not to prosecute has been made, the ground for inadmissibility in Article 17, paragraph 1(b), is fulfilled. If the decision not to prosecute concerns all cases investigated by the truth commission, with amnesty being the only conceivable form of such a decision,[53] the cases would be admissible before the ICC pursuant to Article 17, paragraph 2(a), of the ICC Statute. If the decision is made on a case-by-case basis, the applicability of Article 17, paragraphs 2 or 3, must be examined. Each case should be meticulously reviewed on the basis of the criteria provided in the Statute and considering the specific circumstances of the case without special consideration given to the fact that the case was investigated by a truth commission. The primary concern is whether the decision was made based solely on the merits of the case or whether other factors played a role. Because there is no universally valid formula, this is the only way to determine if a given case, which has been investigated by a truth commission, is admissible before the ICC or not.

3.2.2.2.2   Amnesty powers

To date, the South African Truth and Reconciliation Commission[54] has been the only example of a truth commission with amnesty powers. Thus, its regulations serve as the basis for this analysis even though it is only an example and the cases it investigated do not fall within the jurisdiction of the ICC's *ratione temporis*. Regarding the admissibility test for the ICC, cases that have and have not been amnestied must be distinguished. If a case has not been amnestied, it is to be treated in the same way as the cases investigated by truth commissions without amnesty powers.

The special case is then reduced to the amnesties granted within the scope of truth commissions. Then, the ground for inadmissibility in Article

---

[53] Cf. Law on General Amnesty for the Consolidation of Peace in El Salvador, printed in N.J. Kritz, *Transitional Justice*, Vol. III (Washington DC, United States Institute of Peace Press 1995) 546 ff.

[54] Cf. Schätzler n. 46.

17, paragraph 1(b), of the ICC Statute applies. The case has been investigated and the decision not to prosecute the person concerned has been made. But, in such a case, for the above reasons concerning the inherent aim of amnesties and considering that, in the South African case, amnesty was given in exchange for complete disclosure of the facts (which does not by itself fulfil the goals of criminal justice), it can be argued that this decision not to prosecute had the purpose of shielding the person from criminal liability, making the case admissible before the ICC.[55] It is arguable that this purpose is not related to the decision not to prosecute and that it is not necessarily relevant to the truth commission as an institution because, according to experience, truth commissions are not established to shield people but to permit the reconstruction of the history of controversial past events in a given society.

These considerations lead one to the conclusion that, against the background of the interpretation of the ICC Statute and the principle of complementarity, the ICC should not interfere with current societal processes of dealing with the past as long as they do not cause a violation of human rights. Thus, a case would be inadmissible if a State chose to institute a truth commission which genuinely performed its work. Truth commissions are highly respected as a legitimate step in the national process of dealing with the past. But, if their work has already been done and no prosecutions or criminal investigations are initiated or if the judicial system is unable to prosecute, the case may be admissible if no other State is currently investigating or prosecuting and the case is of sufficient gravity. This conclusion confirms the fact that truth commissions and criminal processes do not exclude each other but rather function complementarily.[56] This con-

---

[55] Contrast J. Dugard, 'Possible Conflicts of Jurisdiction with Truth Commissions', in A. Cassese, P. Gaeta, J. Jones (eds.), *The Rome Statute of the International Criminal Court* (Oxford, Oxford University Press 2002) 693, 699 ff.; Dugard (n. 38) 1014; O'Shea (n. 39) 177 ff.; C. Villa-Vicencio, 'Why Perpetrators Should Not Always Be Prosecuted: Where The International Criminal Court and Truth Commissions Meet', *Emory L J* (2000), 205, 222, quoting Kofi Annan at fn. 78. More sceptical A. Gitti, 'Impunity under National Law and Accountability under International Human Rights Law: Has the Time of a Duty to Prosecute Come?', *Italian Ybk of Intl L* (1999), 64, 83.

[56] Cf. the fundamental *Velásquez Rodríguez case* (*Judgment*) Inter-American Court of Human Rights Series C No. 4 (29 July 1988) para. 166; Inter-American Commission on Human Rights, Annual Report 1997, Report No. 25/98 (1997) para. 68; M.C. Bassiouni,

note continued on p. 139

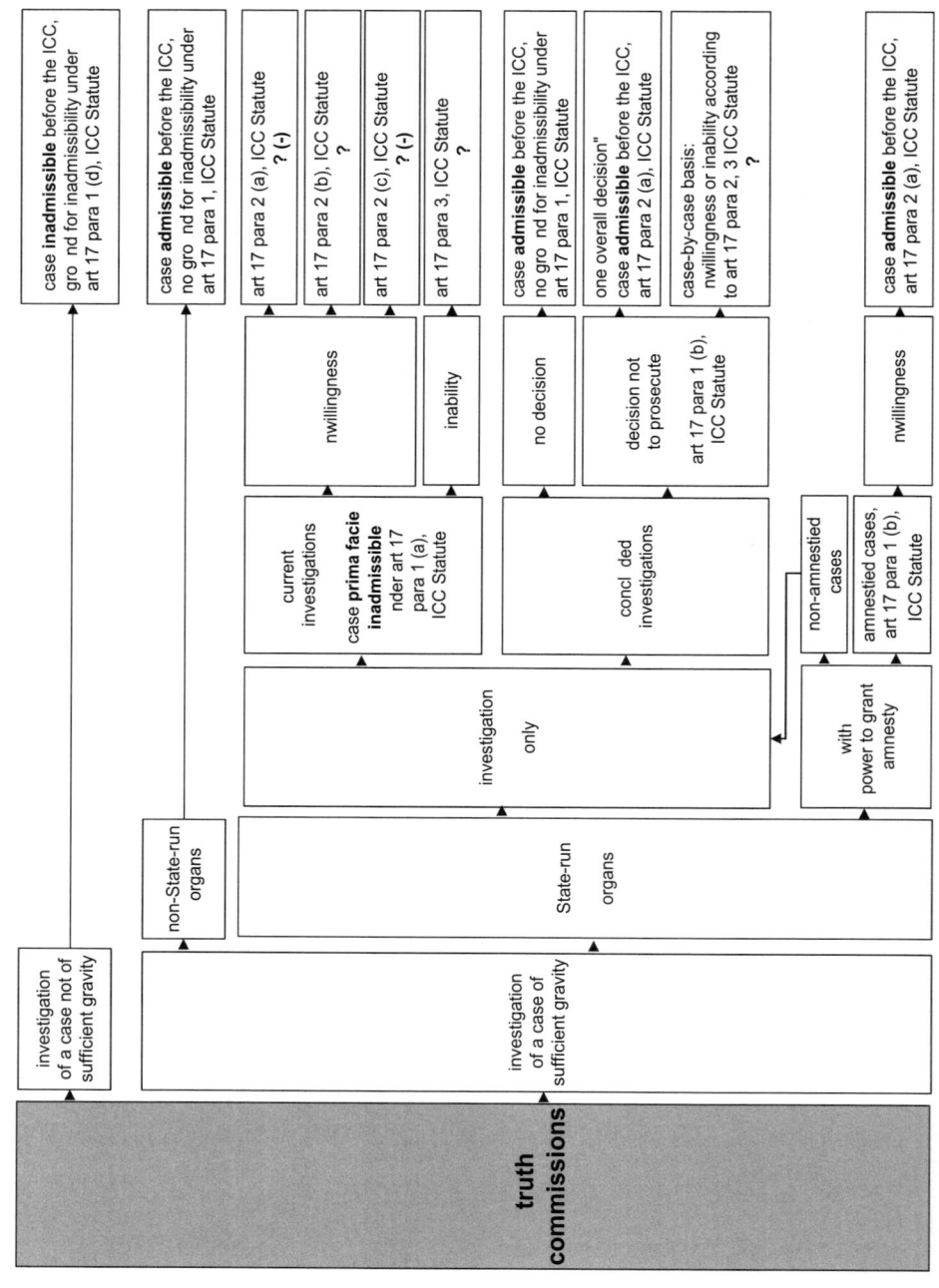

clusion does not imply an underestimation of the work of truth commissions; it simply asserts that they cannot replace criminal prosecutions. Nonetheless, they complement criminal justice by contributing to a clarification of the historical background, and they are necessary and desirable for a State in dealing with past mass crimes.

4. CONCLUSION

The admissibility test is regulated by Article 17 of the ICC Statute. It follows from paragraph 1 that, in principle, each case is considered to be admissible unless a ground for inadmissibility is fulfilled. As the next step in arriving at a final answer to the admissibility test, it is necessary to examine whether an exception to the grounds for inadmissibility has been fulfilled. If so, the case is admissible before the ICC. If not, it is inadmissible and remains exclusively within the jurisdiction of States. The status of cases which have been subject to an amnesty or which are being or have been investigated by a truth commission has to be differentiated for each particular case. Article 17 of the ICC Statute must be applied because no special regulation was foreseen. This article has proposed some guidelines on the matter.

'International Crimes: *Jus Cogens* and *Obligation Erga Omnes*', 59 *Law and Contemporary Problems* (1996), 9, 20; P. Hayner, 'Fifteen Truth Commissions – 1974 to 1994: A Comparative Study', 16 *Human Rights Q* (1994), 597, 605; Hayner (n. 52) 91 ff.; and J. Sarkin, 'The Necessity and Challenges of Establishing a Truth and Reconciliation Commission in Rwanda', 21 *Human Rights Q* (1999), 767, 819 ff.

COMMENTS ON CHAPTER 4 OF CLAUDIA CÁRDENAS ARAVENA

Darryl Robinson*

I have the pleasure of commenting on the paper by Claudia Cárdenas Aravena, chapter 4 in this book, which tackles one of the most interesting and complicated issues in the complementarity discussion, namely the role of amnesties and truth commissions. The paper navigates well through the framework of Article 17 of the Rome Statute, correctly setting out the doctrinal and interpretational nuances. It also has a strict analytical structure which is very useful.

1. THE LIMITED ROLE OF THE 'UNWILLINGNESS' AND 'INABILITY' CRITERIA

I would like to start by highlighting one essential point. It is not even a main theme of the chapter, but I thought it was one of the best articulations of this idea that I have seen. In section 2, she explains, 'as a starting-point the admissibility of each case before the ICC is presumed.'[1] So the starting-point is admissibility, and then a case becomes *inadmissible* only when one of the criteria for inadmissibility is satisfied.[2] This is absolutely correct, it

---

* External Relations and Complementarity Adviser, International Criminal Court, Officer of the Prosecutor, Jurisdiction, Complementarity and Co-operation Division.

[1] Cárdenas Aravena 116.

[2] Art. 17 explains that 'a case is *inadmissible*' (emphasis added) where certain criteria, listed in Art. 17(1)(a), (b) and (c), are met. So the default rule, in the absence of those criteria being satisfied, is admissibility. Rome Statute of the International Criminal Court (Rome Statute) Art. 17 (adopted 17 July 1998, entered into force 1 July 2002) UN Doc. A/CONF. 183/9.

J.K. Kleffner & G. Kor (eds.), Complementary Views on Complementarity
© 2006, T·M·C·ASSER PRESS, The Hague, The Netherlands and the Authors

is extremely well articulated and, surprisingly, it is a point that is frequently misunderstood.

For a long time, commentators, including myself, have been guilty of simplifying the complementarity test. So one hears over and over that 'the ICC will prosecute genocide, crimes against humanity and war crimes, *where national systems are unable or unwilling to do so.*' This is *not* what Article 17 says at all. The 'unwilling and unable' test *only* comes up when one is judging the genuineness of an existent national procedure.

Article 17 actually goes in two steps, as Cárdenas Aravena recognizes. The first step is a purely *empirical* question: Is there a national proceeding or not? The second step is a *normative* question, relevant only if there *is* a national proceeding, in which one must assess whether the State concerned is unwilling or unable genuinely to carry out the proceeding.

If there is no national procedure, then none of the criteria of Article 17, paragraph 1(a), (b) or (c), are satisfied and hence the case is admissible. There is no need to go on to enquire about 'unwillingness', 'inability' or 'genuineness'. For instance, in the situations of the Democratic Republic of Congo and Uganda, many observers are asking whether it is an 'inability' situation or an 'unwillingness' situation. Those questions are irrelevant if there is no national proceeding in place: In such a case it is simply admissible under the plain and clear terms of Article 17.

Thus the more accurate way to summarize Article 17 is the way that Cárdenas Aravena's paper does when it notes: 'The ICC only acts when States do not undertake proceedings or do not do it properly.'[3]

2.   THE DISTINCTION BETWEEN AMNESTIES AND TRUTH COMMISSIONS

The chapter as a whole has a very systematic approach, following a Cartesian or classical logic approach, which is conceptually very tidy. Accordingly, the sections pose a series of clear binary questions, for example, is it a case of sufficient gravity or not, is it a State-run procedure or not, and so on.

---

[3]   Cárdenas Aravena 115.

The structure of the chapter makes such a distinction between truth commissions on the one hand and amnesties on the other. On reflection, I realized that these two branches, truth commissions and amnesties, are not suitable as two branches because they are not mutually exclusive and they are not jointly exhaustive. One can imagine a grid or a quadrant of possibilities. There may be a truth commission, or not. There may be amnesties, or not. The two variables may be independent.

Truth Commission & Amnesty E.g. TC as total solution	Truth Commission & No Amnesty E.g. TC side by side with prosecution
No Truth Commission & Amnesty E.g. 'forget the past'	No Truth Commission & No Amnesty E.g. national prosecutions

One could have a truth commission with no amnesties; that would be a case of truth commissions and prosecutions, operating side by side. One could have a truth commission with amnesties; that means the State has decided just to do the truth commission as a total solution. One could have no truth commission with amnesties; that would be blanket inaction. And one could have prosecutions and no truth commission.

This observation, if accepted, would significantly affect the structure of the chapter, and it might need some thought because there is some overlap in these concepts.

3. THEN WHAT IS THE CORE QUESTION FOR OUR ARTICLE 17 ANALYSIS?

I think the foregoing also forces us to think about the underlying issues of the ICC, amnesties, and truth commissions. If we want to proceed in the binary, logical way, what is the real variable that is pivotal under Article 17? It is not truth commissions *per se* because, if one has a truth commission running and prosecutions are running at the same time, the ICC is obviously content. It is not necessarily amnesties *per se* because, even in the absence of a formal amnesty, there might be a failure of the State to launch proceedings. So the pivotal question under Article 17 appears to be: *Is there a national proceeding or not?*

4. HOW SHOULD 'INVESTIGATION' BE INTERPRETED?
CAN A TRUTH COMMISSION CONDUCT 'INVESTIGATIONS'?

This leads us to another question, what is an 'investigation'? Under Article 17, as Cárdenas Aravena has noted, the term 'proceeding' comprises both national investigations and national prosecutions. So, for an analysis of truth commissions under the complementarity regime, the core question is whether a truth commission's inquiry can be an investigation.

There are many commentators who say that there has to be a *criminal* investigation. Cárdenas Aravena adopts the view, as is my view, that the term 'investigation' can be broader than that. She refers to a systematic inquiry about the facts and the responsibility for the crime. A truth commission inquiry could satisfy this requirement.

Even though I have argued for a broader interpretation of the term 'investigation',[4] now that I have had the benefit of reading the paper and considering its implications, I have had to reconsider my view. I had not considered at length the implications for the analysis of an *ongoing* investigation, as this paper does. Now I would conclude that the interpretation of this word 'investigation' in Article 17 has to include not only a systematic inquiry into the facts and responsibilities, but also at least a *possibility* of a criminal proceeding at the end. Otherwise we will encounter some inexplicable and unsound results in the distinction between ongoing investigations and completed investigations.

Cárdenas Aravena's chapter, following quite logically from the assumptions and interpretations it sets out, distinguishes quite clearly between a current, ongoing investigation and a closed investigation. This distinction is sound because it matches Article 17, paragraph 1(a), current investigation, and Article 17, paragraph 1(b), closed investigation. But I realize that the result was too indefensible a difference in the treatment of these two situations. The completed investigation, in the Cárdenas Aravena analysis, is actually quite easy to pierce. However, the ongoing investigation is very difficult to pierce: One would have to prove unwillingness or inability. This could produce some strange effects. Consider a hypothetical scenario in

---

[4] D. Robinson, 'Serving the Interests of Justice: Amnesties, Truth Commissions and The International Criminal Court', 14 *EJIL* (2003) 481.

which there is a truth commission, but there is also a blanket amnesty in place, and hence the truth commission cannot in the end produce a recommendation to prosecute. At Time One (T_1), when the truth commission is still running, the ICC is held at bay, unless it can prove unwillingness or inability. At Time Two (T_2), once the truth commission is completed, admissibility is easily established.

However, given that the only possible outcome of the truth commission's operation remains, in any event, no prosecutions, then my question is why would the ICC be held at bay under complementarity? Why would it be forced to prove unwilling or unable when there is no chance of prosecutions? And then, when the truth commission finishes, why would the legal issue change so that the ICC no longer has to prove unwilling or unable? From the perspective of the principles of complementarity, there is no significant difference between T_1 and T_2 – at both times there is no possibility of prosecutions.[5]

One rationale for such a different outcome at T_1 and T_2 would be to let an ongoing truth commission do its work. But, if it is an ongoing process that cannot lead to prosecution, the philosophy of complementarity should not require us to defer. The fact that a truth commission is running may be commendable, but for the ICC the major fact would be that there is no possibility of criminal proceedings, so the case should be admissible.

Accordingly, my new thinking, after digesting this chapter, is that I would now still agree that an 'investigation' does not have to be a criminal investigation: It could be an investigation by a truth commission. But I do think there has to be a *possibility* of a criminal prosecution in order to activate the purpose of Article 17. Such an interpretation would be supportable both by a plain meaning analysis and by a contextual and teleological analysis.

I still believe that there is scope to protecting an ongoing investigation by a truth commission. Two things can be done. First there is the interest of justice, where the Prosecutor has the discretion under Article 53, paragraph 1(c), to defer. Another possibility is that the ICC can carry out its operations

---

[5] Of course, there would still be a formal difference in that current investigations are assessed under Art. 17, para. 1(a), and closed investigations are assessed under Art. 17, para. 1(b), but the difference would not be so drastic since the analysis would be similar under either sub-paragraph.

in a way which minimizes interference with the work of the truth commission.

5.   THE LAST QUESTION

In sum, everything about the structure of this chapter is very useful. It gives sound interpretations of these provisions (subject to the observation I have suggested, that the term 'investigation' may require also a possibility of criminal prosecutions), and it provides a very logical formulation of the whole process of analysis.

At the end of the chapter, we reach the most difficult case, where one has, for example, a truth commission that does have discretion either to grant or not to grant an amnesty. The conclusion is that this would have to be judged on a case-by-case basis, and I agree. The big question remains, however, how does one do that? What are the criteria? I would love to see answers to these questions because it may some day become critically relevant for the ICC.

Chapter 5
COMPLEMENTARITY, 'GENUINELY' AND ARTICLE 17: ASSESSING THE BOUNDARIES OF AN EFFECTIVE ICC

*Rod Jensen**

Article 17 of the Rome Statute of the International Criminal Court[1] lies at the heart of the practical operation of the complementary jurisdiction of the ICC. It deals with issues of admissibility and more particularly it specifies the test, framed in exclusionary terms, for determining whether any particular case is inadmissible before the ICC. In so doing, Article 17 gives life to the regime of complementarity contemplated in both paragraph 10 of the Preamble and Article 1 of the Rome Statute.[2]

This chapter focuses upon a particular aspect of Article 17, namely the presence of the word 'genuinely' in the text of the article. One commentator on the Rome Statute enticingly describes the appearance of 'genuinely' in

---

* Doctoral Candidate, Faculty of Law, University of British Columbia, Vancouver, B.C., Canada.

[1] Rome Statute of the International Criminal Court (Rome Statute) (adopted 17 July 1998, entered into force 1 July 2002) UN Doc. A/CONF.183/9. For detailed commentary on the Rome Statute, see R. Lee (ed.), *The International Criminal Court: The Making of the Rome Statute: Issues, Negotiations, Results* (The Hague, Kluwer 1999); O. Triffterer (ed.), *Commentary on the Rome Statute of the International Criminal Court: Observers' Notes, Article by Article* (Baden-Baden, Nomos Verlagsgesellschaft 1999); A. Cassese, P. Gaeta, and J. Jones (eds.), *The Rome Statute of the International Criminal Court: A Commentary*, Vols. 1 and 2 (Oxford, Oxford University Press 2002).

[2] Para. 10 of the Preamble of the Rome Statute (n. 1) reads: 'Emphasizing that the International Criminal Court established under this Statute shall be complementary to national criminal jurisdictions'. Art. 1 reads:
'An International Criminal Court ('the Court') is hereby established. It shall be a permanent institution and shall have the power to exercise its jurisdiction over persons for the most serious crimes of international concern, as referred to in this Statute, and shall be complementary to national criminal jurisdictions. The jurisdiction and functioning of this Court shall be governed by the provisions of this Statute.'

J.K. Kleffner & G. Kor (eds.), Complementary Views on Complementarity
© 2006, T·M·C·ASSER PRESS, The Hague, The Netherlands and the Authors

Article 17 as 'enigmatic'.[3] This is a reference to the fact that unlike the words 'unwillingness' and 'inability', which also appear in Article 17, the word 'genuinely' is not further defined in the Statute and to that extent its interpretation is left 'entirely to the appreciation of the Court.'[4] This makes the word somewhat unique in the context of the Rome Statute because there are few aspects of this multilateral treaty that have been left so open for subsequent interpretation. How the Court will interpret 'genuinely' is therefore an important and intriguing question.

The chapter is divided into two parts. The first part examines the origins of the word 'genuinely' in Article 17 of the Rome Statute. This part argues that 'genuinely' provides a necessary conduit through which the ideal of complementarity can be given effect. It also suggests that 'genuinely' plays a standard-setting role, which consequently allows the ICC to hold States accountable at an international level for their failure to bring the perpetrators of the most serious crimes of international concern to justice. The second part of the chapter considers the historical circumstances that underscore the need to hold States accountable for such failures and traces the quest for the development of a meaningful enforcement mechanism at an international level capable of bringing about greater State accountability. This provides the context for assessing the boundaries of an effective ICC.

1. THE ORIGINS OF 'GENUINELY' IN ARTICLE 17

The issues of admissibility dealt with in Article 17 address the 'politically sensitive and legally complex'[5] relationship between national criminal jurisdictions and the ICC. Creating a balance in this relationship that was workable for the purposes of an effective ICC and yet acceptable from the point of view of States protective of the role of their national criminal jurisdictions was an essential feature of the discussions and negotiations that led to the inclusion of Article 17 in its present form in the Rome Statute. The

---

[3] W. Schabas, *An Introduction to the International Criminal Court* (Cambridge, Cambridge University Press 2001) 67.

[4] Ibid.

[5] J. Holmes, 'The Principle of Complementarity', in *The International Criminal Court: The Making of the Rome Statute* (n. 1) 41.

solution offered by the Statute is based upon the concepts of unwillingness and inability. The Preparatory Committee[6] arrived at this solution during the preparatory phase of the drafting of the Rome Statute and, while it was tinkered with during the negotiation of the Statute at the Rome Conference, no substantial impediment was raised to these concepts remaining at the heart of Article 17.[7] It was also during the preparatory phase of the drafting of the Rome Statute that the first mention was made of the word 'genuinely' in Article 17.

In order to understand more completely how and why the Preparatory Committee arrived at its formulation of Article 17, it is first necessary to examine in brief detail the formulation that was offered by the International Law Commission (ILC) in its draft statute for an international criminal court, which formed the foundation of the Preparatory Committee's consideration,[8] and also to consider the comments of the *Ad Hoc* Committee, which was formed by the United Nations General Assembly in 1995 to review and comment upon the ILC draft statute.[9]

1.1 The ILC draft statute

The ILC produced a draft statute comprising sixty articles grouped into eight parts.[10] The ILC draft statute commenced with a preamble setting out

---

[6] The Preparatory Committee on the Establishment of an International Criminal Court was established by the United Nations General Assembly to prepare a 'widely acceptable consolidated draft text of a convention for an international criminal court as a next step towards consideration by a conference of plenipotentiaries.' 'Establishment of International Criminal Court', UNGA Res 50/46 (18 December 1995) UN Doc A/RES/50/46.

[7] Holmes (n. 5) 51-56.

[8] The ILC, an expert body whose function is to develop and codify international law, had been examining, under the direction of the General Assembly of the United Nations, the possibility of creating an International Criminal Court from as early as 1948. J. Pejic, 'Creating A Permanent International Criminal Court: The Obstacles to Independence and Effectiveness', 29 *Columbia Human Rights L R* (1998) 291, 294-299.

[9] 'Report of the *Ad Hoc* Committee on the Establishment of an International Criminal Court' (Report of the *Ad Hoc* Committee) (6 September 1995) GAOR 50th Sess Supp No. 22 (A/50/22).

[10] International Law Commission, 'Report of the International Law Commission on the Work of its 46th Session'(ILC Report) 43 para. 91 (2 May-22 July 1994) GAOR 49th Sess Supp No. 10 (A/49/10).

the main purposes of the statute. Included in the preamble was a statement emphasizing that the proposed ICC is intended to 'be complementary to national criminal justice systems in cases where such trial procedures may not be available or may be ineffective.'[11] This short statement heralded the importance of the principle of complementarity for the purposes of the statute. This importance was underscored in the commentary of the ILC accompanying the preamble, which noted:

> 'The emphasis is thus on the Court as a body which will complement existing national jurisdictions and existing procedures for international judicial cooperation in criminal matters and which is not intended to exclude the existing jurisdiction of national courts, or to affect the right of States to seek extradition and other forms of international judicial assistance under existing arrangements.'[12]

In this way, the ILC conceptualized an ICC that could complement existing national criminal justice systems without assuming primacy over them.

Of central importance to the operation of the ICC proposed by the ILC was the rationale that the Court would only be required to operate in instances where the trial procedures of a national criminal justice system were unavailable or ineffective. In these instances the ICC would complement the national criminal justice system by providing an alternative forum in which an alleged perpetrator could be brought to justice. However, by extending the reach of the ICC beyond situations in which trial procedures were not available to situations where trial procedures were ineffective, the ILC contemplated that the Court would be able to intervene in cases that had already been or were being investigated by national authorities. While this gave the Court a potentially greater field of operation than that which would have existed had its role been confined merely to those situations where trial procedures were unavailable, it also raised the potential for the ICC to encroach upon the sovereign prerogatives of States by allowing the Court to engage in a review of the effectiveness of the investigative and prosecutorial processes of national criminal justice systems.

---

[11] Ibid. 69.
[12] Ibid. 44.

To a great extent, this potential was realized in the article of the ILC draft statute that gave effect to the vision the ILC had of complementarity. This article identified those cases that would be inadmissible before the ICC because of prior or continuing State involvement.[13] According to the article, a case would be inadmissible in three alternative circumstances. First, it would be inadmissible if it had been duly investigated by a State with jurisdiction over it and the State had made a decision not to proceed with prosecution. Secondly, it would be inadmissible if a State with jurisdiction over it was investigating it. And thirdly, it would be inadmissible if it was of insufficient gravity to justify further action by the Court. However, in relation to the first two circumstances, the draft statute went further. Where a State had investigated a case and had made a decision not to proceed with prosecution, the article gave the Court authority to determine whether that decision was 'apparently well-founded'.[14] Additionally, in circumstances where a case was still under investigation by a State, the article gave the Court the power to intervene if it felt there was reason to do so.[15]

The importance of this formulation for the purpose of the future drafting of Article 17 was that it made clear that the ILC intended the Court to be an institution endowed with the ability to intervene in cases where States had acted or were acting and, through such intervention, to ensure that the national proceedings were effective for the purpose of bringing to justice those accused of crimes within the scope of the draft statute. At the same time, however, the ILC contemplated that the Court would only deal with cases

---

[13] Art. 35 of the ILC draft statute, in ILC Report (n. 10) 105, provides:
'Article 35
Issues of admissibility
The Court may ... decide, having regard to the purposes of this Statute set out in the preamble, that a case before it is inadmissible on the ground that the crime in question:
a) has been duly investigated by a State with jurisdiction over it, and the decision of that State not to proceed to a prosecution is apparently well-founded;
b) is under investigation by a State which has or may have jurisdiction over it, and there is no reason for the Court to take any further action for the time being with respect to the crime; or
c) is not of such gravity to justify further action by the court.'
[14] Ibid. 105 (Art. 35a).
[15] Ibid. 105 (Art. 35b).

in circumstances where, in light of the preamble, 'it was really desirable to do so'.[16]

1.2   Review and comment by the *Ad Hoc* Committee

Both the preamble and the article on admissibility in the ILC draft statute attracted the attention of the *Ad Hoc* Committee during its review of the ILC draft in 1995.[17] In relation to the preamble, some States felt that it did not go far enough, preferring instead that it create a stronger presumption in favour of national criminal jurisdictions having primary responsibility to prosecute violations of their laws, while other States argued that the ICC should assume primary jurisdiction with national courts exercising concurrent jurisdiction.[18] In relation to the article on admissibility, some States felt uncomfortable about the ICC being granted the power to act like an appeals tribunal, examining and commenting upon the effectiveness of domestic investigative and prosecutorial processes. The preferred approach, it was argued, was that such examination should take place in domestic courts or perhaps through a process of review before the United Nations Security Council.[19]

The end result was that, while the *Ad Hoc* Committee saw complementarity as an essential element in the establishment of the ICC, it concluded that further elaboration was required 'so that its implications for the substantive provisions of the draft statute could be fully understood.'[20] The opportunity for such elaboration was presented when the Preparatory Committee began its consideration of the ILC draft statute in 1996.

1.3   Consideration by the Preparatory Committee

The Preparatory Committee first discussed complementarity at its March-April session in 1996, and it soon became apparent that there existed widely

---

[16]   Ibid. 105 (commentary to Art. 35).

[17]   Report of the *Ad Hoc* Committee (n. 9); S. Williams, 'Article 17: Issues of Admissibility', in O. Triffterer (ed.), *Commentary on the Rome Statute* (n. 1) 383, 385-386.

[18]   Williams (n. 17) 386.

[19]   Ibid.

[20]   Report of the *Ad Hoc* Committee (n. 9) para. 29.

divergent views on how complementarity should feature in the draft statute.[21] Some delegates expressed a concern that the approach set out in the preamble to the ILC draft statute, based as it was upon the unavailability and ineffectiveness of national criminal justice systems, was too vague, while others argued that it was too intrusive.[22] Some delegates sought further definition of the words 'unavailable' and 'ineffective', while others sought to have them omitted altogether.[23] In order to be acceptable to a large number of the delegates, it was apparent that the references to complementarity in the draft statute would have to allow for a 'proper balance'[24] in 'the jurisdictional relationship between the International Criminal Court and national authorities, including national courts.'[25]

Having discussed complementarity in the March-April session of 1996, the Preparatory Committee did not again discuss it in detail until its August session in 1997. At the commencement of this session, the Preparatory Committee decided to conduct its work through two working groups: the Working Group on Complementarity and Trigger Mechanisms and the Working Group on Procedural Matters.[26] However, while the discussion on complementarity began in plenary, it soon moved into informal consultations coordinated by the acting head of the Canadian delegation, Mr. John Holmes.[27] These informal consultations continued over the course of a week

---

[21] 'Report of the Preparatory Committee on the Establishment of an International Criminal Court Vol 1 (Proceedings of the Preparatory Committee during March-April and August 1996)' (Report of the Preparatory Committee) paras. 153-178 (13 September 1996) GAOR 51st Session Supp No. 22 (A/51/22).

[22] Holmes (n. 5) 45.

[23] Report of the Preparatory Committee (n. 21) para. 161.

[24] Ibid. para. 153.

[25] Ibid.

[26] UN General Assembly Preparatory Committee on the Establishment of an International Criminal Court 'Decisions Taken by the Preparatory Committee at Its Session Held from 4 to 15 August 1997' (14 August 1997) 1 para. 1 UN Doc A/AC.249/1997/L.8/Rev.1.

[27] Holmes (n. 5) 45; 'Report on Working Group 3 Complementarity and Trigger Mechanisms: Committee on the Establishment of an International Criminal Court' (August 4-15 1997) <http://www.iccnow.org/romearchive/documentsreports/4PrepCmt/4PrepCmtWork Grp3Summary.pdf> (20 July 2005). While the process of informal consultations may have assisted the Working Group on Complementarity to arrive at a workable solution on the issue of complementarity, an unfortunate consequence is that there now exists little by way of a formal record indicating what transpired during the negotiations that led to the production of the modified draft article.

and involved 'intense negotiations'[28] but they culminated with the production of a modified draft article on complementarity that was subsequently
approved by the Preparatory Committee at the end of the August session.[29]

At the center of this modified draft article was a shift in emphasis from
the ILC conception of an ICC, whose jurisdictional authority was based
upon the unavailability and ineffectiveness of a State's trial procedures, to a
Preparatory Committee conception of an ICC, whose jurisdictional authority was based upon the unwillingness and inability of a State to carry out an
investigation or prosecution. Pursuant to the approach of the Preparatory
Committee, the ICC would not assume jurisdiction over a case unless the
State with jurisdiction over it was either unwilling or unable to carry out the
investigation or prosecution. In each instance, whether through unwillingness or inability, the end result would be 'a defect in the approach taken by
the State which inevitably, if left to its conclusion, would lead to a travesty
of justice.'[30]

However, a logical consequence of this approach is that, in order to remedy a defect brought about by a State's unwillingness or inability to investigate or to prosecute a case, the ICC must first identify that a defect actually
exists, and, in order to do that, it must undertake a review of the particular
factors underlying the State's unwillingness or inability to investigate or
prosecute. A major point of discussion in the informal consultations was
agreeing upon an approach by which the Court could do this in a meaningful way while at the same time not encroaching to an unacceptable extent
upon the prerogative rights of States to exercise police power and penal law
through their own systems of law enforcement and national courts.

As in the *Ad Hoc* Committee, many delegations 'were sensitive to the
potential for the Court to function as a kind of court of appeal, passing
judgments on the decisions and proceedings of national judicial systems.'[31]
However, it was also understood that, in order to be effective, the Court had

---

[28] Holmes (n. 5) 46.

[29] Ibid. 46; UN General Assembly 'Report of the Working Group on Complementarity
and Trigger Mechanism' (14 August 1997) UN Doc A/AC.249/1997/L.6.

[30] J. Holmes, 'Complementarity: National Courts versus the ICC', in A. Cassese, P.
Gaeta and J. Jones (eds.), *The Rome Statute of the International Criminal Court: A Commentary* (n. 1) 667, 674.

[31] Holmes (n. 5) 49.

to be able to look behind the actions of States relating to particular investigations or prosecutions to determine whether those actions had been or were being carried out in a way that respected the main aim of the Rome Statute, which was to ensure that the most serious crimes of international concern did not go unpunished. What was required then was a standard that could be applied by the Court when assessing the unwillingness or inability of a State to investigate or prosecute a case. Without such a standard it would have been possible for a State to avoid the jurisdiction of the Court by, for example, simply initiating a fraudulent investigation into a case in order to demonstrate that it was neither unwilling nor unable to investigate or prosecute the matter, and there would be nothing that the Court could do to challenge the motivation behind that action.[32]

Accepting that such a standard was necessary, the delegations remained anxious to ensure that it should remain as objective as possible. For this reason, a number of terms were rejected during discussions because they were thought to be too subjective. These included 'ineffective', 'diligently', 'sufficient grounds',[33] 'apparently well-founded' (as used by the ILC), and 'effectively' (which was also considered too judgmental).[34] The term 'good faith' was also rejected on the basis that it was thought to be too narrow.[35]

Eventually the word 'genuinely' was seized upon, which, according to the coordinator, 'captured the concerns of some delegations by being the least subjective concept considered. It excluded elements of efficiency, while at the same time being more precise than sufficient or reasonable grounds.'[36] Consequently it was agreed to by the delegations and included in Article 17 so that, if a case was being investigated or prosecuted by a State which had jurisdiction over it, the case would be inadmissible before the ICC unless the State was unwilling or unable *genuinely* to carry out the investigation or prosecution (emphasis added),[37] and similarly, if a case had already been

---

[32] ICC Office of the Prosecutor, 'Informal Expert Paper: The Principle of Complementarity in Practice' (2003) <http://www.icc-cpi.int/library/organs/otp/complementarity.pdf> (20 July 2005).

[33] Holmes (n. 30) 674.

[34] Holmes (n. 5) 49.

[35] Holmes (n. 30) 674.

[36] Ibid.

[37] Rome Statute (n. 1) Art. 17 para. 1a.

investigated by a State which had jurisdiction over it and the State had decided not to prosecute the person concerned, the case would be inadmissible before the ICC unless the decision resulted from the unwillingness or inability of the State *genuinely* to prosecute (emphasis added).[38]

In light of this drafting history, the role of 'genuinely' in Article 17 is to set a minimum standard for States to adhere to when carrying out either an investigation or prosecution of a case involving a crime within the subject-matter jurisdiction of the ICC or when deciding whether to prosecute such a case.[39] If a State is unwilling or unable to meet this minimum standard, then it risks forfeiting jurisdiction over the case to the ICC. In this way the word 'genuinely' acts as a conduit through which the ideal of complementarity in the Rome Statute is given effect because it offers States the first opportunity to investigate and prosecute allegations of crimes within the subject-matter jurisdiction of the ICC and it is only when a State is unwilling or unable to meet the minimum standard that the ICC can consider intervening. This approach protects States from an overly intrusive ICC by restricting the ability of the Court to embark upon a broad, discretionary examination of the nature and extent of a State's investigation or prosecution in a particular case.

The protection offered to States through this approach was enhanced by the Preparatory Committee's inclusion in Article 17 of detailed criteria that the Court is mandated to use when determining unwillingness[40] or inability.[41] In relation to unwillingness, the criteria describe situations in which it could be said that a State has failed to act genuinely in carrying out its investigation or prosecution or in deciding not to prosecute a matter that has been investigated. In relation to inability, the criteria describe situations that might impede the ability of a State to act genuinely in carrying out its investigation or prosecution or in making the decision not to prosecute a matter that has been investigated. The detailed nature of the criteria makes it unlikely that the Court could go outside of them when making an assessment of unwillingness or inability.[42]

---

[38] Ibid. Art. 17 para. 1b.
[39] The crimes within the subject-matter jurisdiction of the Court are the crime of genocide, crimes against humanity and war crimes. Ibid. Art. 5 para. 1.
[40] Ibid. Art. 17 para. 2.
[41] Ibid. Art. 17 para. 3.
[42] Holmes (n. 30) 674-675.

However, while the presence of the word 'genuinely' in Article 17 serves to protect States from unwarranted intrusion by the ICC by providing a minimum standard for State conduct, it also serves to make States accountable if they fail to observe the minimum standard. This is an important feature of the complementary regime of the ICC because, at a macroscopic level, the Rome Statute is only concerned with the individual criminal responsibility of persons who commit the most serious crimes of international concern.[43] However, at a microscopic level, the Statute has far greater reach because it allows States to be held accountable for their failure to enforce individual criminal responsibility for these crimes at a national level. Much of the credit for bringing about this process of accountability must be given to the malleable presence of the word 'genuinely' in Article 17, which serves both to protect States and yet, at the same time, to make them accountable.

At the conclusion of a week of informal consultations, the Working Group on Complementarity and Trigger Mechanisms was able to put forward a modified draft article on complementarity that was subsequently approved by the Preparatory Committee at the end of the August session.[44] The draft article, containing the word 'genuinely', then took its place in the draft statute for consideration at the Rome Conference.[45]

1.4   The Rome Conference

The draft article on admissibility presented by the Preparatory Committee to the Rome Conference represented a 'delicately balanced compromise.'[46] If delegates to the Conference sought to reopen the substance of the provision, there was a real possibility that they might upset the balance, thereby

---

[43]   Rome Statute (n. 1) Art. 25.

[44]   Holmes (n. 5) 46; Report of the Working Group on Complementarity and Trigger Mechanism (n. 29).

[45]   The draft article on complementarity was 'left untouched' by the Bureau of Preparatory Committee at its special meeting in Zutphen, the Netherlands in January 1998. Holmes (n. 5) 51; cf. L. Sadat, *The International Criminal Court And The Transformation of International Law: Justice For The New Millennium* (New York, Transnational Publishers 2001) 124.

[46]   Williams (n. 17) 390.

causing the package on complementary jurisdiction to fold entirely.[47] The object, therefore, was to identify what changes could be accommodated without undertaking a wholesale re-evaluation of the substance of the article. Ultimately, only a few changes were made to the draft article as presented by the Preparatory Committee and none of these modified the presence of the word 'genuinely' in the article.[48]

The final version of Article 17 incorporated into the Rome Statute reads as follows:

'Article 17
Issues of admissibility
1. Having regard to paragraph 10 of the Preamble and article 1, the Court shall determine that a case is inadmissible where:
a) The case is being investigated or prosecuted by a State which has jurisdiction over it, unless the State is unwilling or unable genuinely to carry out the investigation or prosecution;
b) The case has been investigated by a State which has jurisdiction over it and the State has decided not to prosecute the person concerned, unless the decision resulted from the unwillingness or inability of the State genuinely to prosecute;
c) The person concerned has already been tried for conduct which is the subject of the complaint, and a trial by the court is not permitted under article 20, paragraph 3;[49]
d) The case is not of sufficient gravity to justify further action by the Court.
2. In order to determine unwillingness in a particular case, the Court shall consider, having regard to the principles of due process recognized by international law, whether one or more of the following exist as applicable:
a) The proceedings were or are being undertaken or the national decision was

---

[47] Ibid.

[48] Holmes (n. 5) 51-56.

[49] Rome Statute (n. 1) Art. 20 para. 3:
'No person who has been tried by another court for conduct also proscribed under article 6, 7 or 8 shall be tried by the Court with respect to the same conduct unless the proceedings in the other court:
(a) Were for the purpose of shielding the person concerned from criminal responsibility for crimes within the jurisdiction of the Court; or
(b) Otherwise were not conducted independently or impartially in accordance with the norms of due process recognized by international law and were conducted in a manner which, in the circumstances, was inconsistent with an intent to bring the person concerned to justice.'

made for the purpose of shielding the person concerned from criminal responsibility for crimes within the jurisdiction of the Court referred to in article 5;
b) There has been an unjustified delay in the proceedings which in the circumstances is inconsistent with an intent to bring the person concerned to justice;
c) The proceedings were not or are not being conducted independently or impartially, and they were or are being conducted in a manner which, in the circumstances, is inconsistent with an intent to bring the person to justice.
3. In order to determine inability in a particular case, the Court shall consider
whether, due to a total or substantial collapse or unavailability of its national
judicial system, the State is unable to obtain the accused or the necessary evidence and testimony or otherwise unable to carry out its proceedings.'[50]

1.5 Genuinely and beyond

One of the curious features of the appearance of the word 'genuinely' in
Article 17, as set out above, is its lack of a definition, especially when
compared to the words 'unwillingness' and 'inability'. It will therefore almost certainly fall to the ICC to interpret the meaning of 'genuinely' when
considering issues of admissibility pursuant to Article 17. In the absence of
any definition in the Statute, the Elements of Crimes or the Rules of Procedure and Evidence, which are the first tier of applicable law for the ICC,[51]
the Court will be bound by Article 31, paragraph 1, of the Vienna Convention on the Law of Treaties, which requires that a 'treaty be interpreted in
good faith in accordance with the ordinary meaning to be given to the terms
of the treaty in their context and in the light of its object and purpose.'[52]
Using these criteria, it is possible to envisage how the Court might interpret
'genuinely'.

When considering the inclusion of 'genuinely' in Article 17, the coordinator of the informal consultations consulted the Oxford English Dictio-
nary for a definition of the word and was impressed by that aspect of the
definition that read: 'Having the supposed character, not sham or feigned.'[53]

---

[50] Ibid. Art. 17.
[51] Ibid. Art. 21 para. 1.
[52] Vienna Convention on the Law of Treaties Art. 31 para. 1 (opened for signature 23
May 1969, entered into force 27 January 1980) 1155 *UNTS* 331.
[53] Holmes (n. 5) 50, quoting.

This definition is consistent with the object and purpose of the Rome Statute, which, ultimately, is to ensure that the most serious crimes of international concern do not go unpunished. If a State carries out an investigation or prosecution or makes a decision not to prosecute in a manner that is sham or feigned, then it is unlikely that this object and purpose can be achieved.

In the context of Article 17, 'genuinely' therefore compels States to carry out investigations and prosecutions and to make decisions about whether to prosecute in a manner consistent with the aims of the Rome Statute. These aims are conveniently set out in the preamble to the Statute and are directed at bringing an end to impunity for the perpetrators of the most serious crimes of international concern to the international community as a whole. Any investigation, prosecution or decision not to prosecute that is made in a manner inconsistent with these aims will be susceptible to review by the ICC.

This approach emphasizes one of the most important features of Article 17, which is its ability to allow States to be held accountable for their failure to enforce individual criminal responsibility at a national level. The inclusion of this feature in the Rome Statute is a bold initiative and one that has the potential to bring an end to the impunity that has for so long been enjoyed by many of the perpetrators of the most serious crimes of international concern. The next part of this chapter considers the historical circumstances that underscore the need to hold States accountable for failing to enforce individual criminal responsibility at the national level.

2. INDIVIDUAL CRIMINAL RESPONSIBILITY AND STATE ACCOUNTABILITY IN INTERNATIONAL LAW

International law has traditionally been concerned with governing relations between States, and, therefore, until the conclusion of the Second World War, the only active subjects of international law were States.[54] However, this perception changed with the advent of the International Military Tribu-

---

[54] N. Jorgensen, *The Responsibility of States for International Crimes* (Oxford, Oxford University Press 2000) 139.

nal sitting at Nuremberg. Suddenly the individual became a subject of international law through the Tribunal's observation that individuals could be held responsible for crimes against international law and could be punished accordingly.[55]

2.1 Human rights and individual criminal responsibility

The Nuremberg Tribunal's observation regarding individual criminal responsibility provided a springboard for the development of international human rights law because 'much of the international community came to conclude that a state's treatment of its citizens in peacetime was appropriate for general international regulation.'[56] This was an important advancement because historically individuals within the territorial boundaries of States only enjoyed such protection as their State of nationality was willing to extend to them and they had neither rights nor recourse on an international plane against abuses committed upon them by their own governments.[57] However, with the realization that the individual could be viewed as a subject of international law came the understanding that individuals should be entitled to certain rights at an international level and also that those rights should be protected from abuse by the actions of governments within States.

A major development in the years immediately following the Second World War was the adoption of the Universal Declaration of Human Rights[58] by the United Nations in 1948. The Universal Declaration focused upon the rights of individuals and the respect that ought to be accorded to those rights by the international community. In so doing, it laid a foundation for the

---

[55] See, generally, G. Triggs, 'National Prosecutions of War Crimes and the Rule of Law', in H. Durham and T. McCormack (eds.), *The Changing Face of Conflict and the Efficacy of International Humanitarian Law* (The Hague, Kluwer Law International 1999) 176.

[56] S. Ratner and J. Abrams, *Accountability For Human Rights Atrocities In International Law* (Oxford, Clarendon Press 1997) 6.

[57] T. Buergenthal, 'International Human Rights in an Historical Perspective', in J. Symonides (ed.), *Human Rights: Concepts and Standards* (Aldershot, Dartmouth Publishing 2000) 5.

[58] Universal Declaration of Human Rights (adopted 10 December 1948) UNGA Res 217 A(III).

claim that States could no longer view human rights as being purely domestic in nature.[59] At the same time, it reinforced the idea that individuals were capable subjects of international law. However, while the Universal Declaration proclaimed the existence of certain rights, it did not itself create any mechanism capable of enforcing those rights at an international level. The absence of such a mechanism reflects both the declaratory function and the non-binding nature of the Universal Declaration, each of which made it impractical for the Declaration to attempt to put in place any means of enforcement beyond the voluntary actions of States.

However, at around this same time, the international community was considering concrete means by which individuals could be protected at an international level from human rights abuses and from grave breaches of humanitarian law. These considerations arose as a response to the horrors that had been witnessed in the Second World War and, building upon the Nuremberg experience, prompted the international community to search for meaningful ways to bring the perpetrators of such horrors to justice. As a consequence, the United Nations adopted in quick succession the Genocide Convention,[60] dealing with human rights law, and the Geneva Conventions,[61] dealing with humanitarian law, each of which sought to protect vulnerable individuals and to establish criminal responsibility for individuals violating their provisions. In particular, the Genocide Convention contemplated that persons charged with genocide would be brought to justice in national courts or, if it could be formed, an international penal tribunal,[62]

---

[59] Buergenthal (n. 57) 12.

[60] Convention on the Prevention and Punishment of the Crime of Genocide (opened for signature 9 December 1948, entered into force 12 January 1951) 78 *UNTS* 277 (Genocide Convention).

[61] Geneva Convention for the Amelioration of the Condition of the Wounded and Sick in Armed Forces in the Field (opened for signature 12 August 1949, entered into force 21 October 1950) 75 *UNTS* 31 (Geneva Convention I); Geneva Convention for the Amelioration of the Condition of Wounded, Sick and Shipwrecked Members of the Armed Forces at Sea (opened for signature 12 August 1949, entered into force 21 October 1951) 75 *UNTS* 85 (Geneva Convention II); Geneva Convention Relative to the Treatment of Prisoners of War (opened for signature 12 August 1949; entered into force 21 October 1950) 75 *UNTS* 135 (Geneva Convention III); Geneva Convention Relative to the Protection of Civilian Persons in Time of War (opened for signature 12 August 1949, entered into force 21 October 1950) 75 *UNTS* 278 (Geneva Convention IV).

[62] Genocide Convention (n. 60) Art. 6.

while the Geneva Conventions called upon Contracting States to search out and bring to justice any person or persons, regardless of nationality, who committed grave breaches of the Geneva Conventions and to prosecute them in their own courts or to deliver them to States that were willing to undertake the prosecutions.[63] These conventions increased the level of individual criminal responsibility at an international level for serious violations of human rights and humanitarian law and provided an opportunity for States to further the cause of bringing the perpetrators of such violations to justice.

2.2 Searching for State accountability

Historically, however, the increased level of individual criminal responsibility did not equate to a proportional increase in the number of prosecutions for serious violations in the post-War years, despite there being numerous instances that were ripe for attention. The fundamental reason for this lack of proportionality was simply that while treaty-based mechanisms like the Genocide and Geneva Conventions made individuals criminally responsible for breaches of their provisions, they were unable to offer any effective means for ensuring that States would actually honor their commitment to bring individuals accused of such breaches to justice.

The international penal tribunal contemplated by the Genocide Convention did not come to fruition, and this left States to assume the responsibility for investigating and prosecuting alleged violations when they arose. However, one of the intrinsic characteristics of the Westphalian system of States is that each recognized State within the system is entitled to make its own policy choices at a domestic level, free from external intervention by other recognized States within the same system.[64] A concomitant of this approach is that each State has full authority over activities occurring within its own borders and is therefore free to structure its relationship with its citizens as it deems appropriate.

---

[63] Geneva Convention I (n. 61) Art. 49; Geneva Convention II (n. 61) Art. 50; Geneva Convention III (n. 61) Art. 129; Geneva Convention IV (n. 61) Art. 146.

[64] D. Held and others, *Global Transformations, Politics, Economics and Culture* (Cambridge, Polity Press 1999) 32-49.

The irony of this situation, in the years following the creation of the Universal Declaration and the Genocide and Geneva Conventions, was that States could make commitments at an international level to treaties and other international agreements that sought to protect individuals from serious violations of human rights and humanitarian laws but then fail to honor those commitments at a national level, comfortable in the knowledge that other States within the system would be unlikely to intervene to remedy that failure for fear of intruding upon the State's entitlement to pursue its own policy choices free from the threat of external intervention. Within this system 'order and not justice' informed the dealings between States to the detriment of the protection of individuals within those States.[65]

A further consequence of this approach was that States could not be held accountable in any meaningful way for failing to bring to justice those responsible for violations of human rights and humanitarian law occurring within their borders, and this fuelled the notion that the perpetrators of the most serious crimes of international concern could act with impunity, particularly in situations where the violations were sanctioned by the government within the State or carried out in pursuit of a government policy. What was lacking in this environment was a meaningful enforcement mechanism capable of holding States (and more particularly, the governments within States) accountable for domestic policy choices that allowed violations to occur and then afforded the violators impunity.

2.3 Developing a meaningful enforcement mechanism

Developing a meaningful enforcement mechanism during the period of the Cold War, when the bipolar interests of the major superpowers clouded international affairs, proved to be an unrealistic project. Therefore, it was not until the end of the Cold War in the late 1980s that conditions became ripe for seriously considering the possibility of establishing an enforcement mechanism at an international level that might be capable of bringing about greater State accountability for activities occurring within State borders.

---

[65] M. Wind, 'Legal Globalization and the New Human Rights Regime: Human Rights in a Post-Sovereign World', in S. Krishna-Hensel (ed.), *The New Millennium: Challenges and Strategies For A Globalizing World* (Aldershot, Ashgate Publishing 2000) 265.

The first major steps in this direction came with the formation, in the early 1990s, of the international criminal tribunals to try alleged serious breaches of humanitarian law arising from the conflicts in the former Yugoslavia (ICTY)[66] and Rwanda (ICTR).[67] These tribunals were created by the United Nations Security Council, acting under its Chapter VII authority, to maintain or restore international peace and security, and they were the first real attempt since the Nuremberg trials to create an international enforcement mechanism for the purpose of bringing to justice the perpetrators of gross violations of humanitarian law.[68] The creation of these tribunals was therefore an extraordinary and unprecedented measure for both the Security Council and the international community and underscored the enormous sense of change that accompanied the end of the Cold War. However, while the tribunals can be regarded as international enforcement mechanisms, they cannot be regarded as enforcement mechanisms of general application.

In this regard, the tribunals are not permanent institutions. They are *ad hoc* creations of the Security Council and the decisions of the Security Council that created them are decisions of specific application in that they do not impose general obligations on other Member States of the United Nations. This is reflected in the fact that the jurisdiction of each tribunal is limited both territorially and temporally, which consequently gives each of the tribunals a very restricted field of operation.[69] However, the creation of the

---

[66] International Tribunal for the Prosecution of Persons Responsible for Serious Violations of International Humanitarian Law Committed in the Territory of the Former Yugoslavia since 1991. The ICTY was established by Security Council Resolution 827 (25 May 1993) UNSCOR 48th Sess 3217th Meeting UN Doc S/RES/827.

[67] International Criminal Tribunal for the Prosecution of Persons Responsible for Genocide and Other Serious Violations of International Humanitarian Law Committed in the Territory of Rwanda and Rwandan Citizens Responsible for Genocide and Other Such Violations Committed in the Territory of Neighbouring States, between 1 January 1994 and 31 December 1994. The ICTR was established by Security Council Resolution 955 (8 November 1994) UNSCOR 49th Sess 3453rd Meeting UN Doc S/RES/955.

[68] Art. 39 of Chapter VII of the Charter of the United Nations gives the Security Council authority to make recommendations or to decide what measures shall be taken to maintain or restore international peace and security. B. Simma and others (eds.), *The Charter of the United Nations: A Commentary* (Oxford, Oxford University Press 1994) 393-397.

[69] In the case of the ICTY, the territorial jurisdiction extends only to the territory of the former Socialist Federal Republic of Yugoslavia and jurisdiction is temporally limited to a

tribunals advanced the idea of holding accountable the perpetrators of the most serious crimes of international concern and focused public opinion on the need for a more permanent institution to deal with such individuals. This in turn served as a catalyst for the formation of the ICC.[70]

The ICC, however, is distinguishable from the international criminal tribunals in a number of fundamental ways. First, the ICC is a permanent international institution rather than a temporary *ad hoc* response to a particular event. This means that the ICC will have a continuous international presence and that it will not rely exclusively upon the agency of the United Nations Security Council in order to pursue its mandate. Secondly, the jurisdiction of the ICC is prospective as opposed to the jurisdiction of the international tribunals, which in each instance is retrospective. This means that the ICC will be placed and available to adjudicate future events, if and when they arise, as opposed to only having a limited life for the purpose of adjudicating an event that is temporally and territorially isolated. Thirdly, the jurisdiction of the ICC is complementary to national criminal jurisdictions, whereas the international criminal tribunals share concurrent jurisdiction with the respective national courts and can claim primacy over those courts at any stage in the procedure.[71] This means that States, and not the ICC, will bear the primary responsibility for investigating and prosecuting the perpetrators of crimes within the subject-matter jurisdiction of the ICC.

2.4   The ICC as a meaningful enforcement mechanism

These distinguishing characteristics make the ICC a more permanent and ongoing enforcement mechanism than the international criminal tribunals, but it is the complementary nature of the ICC's jurisdiction that has the most potential to ensure that the Court can be regarded as a truly meaning-

---

period beginning 1 January 1991. Statute of the ICTY Arts. 1 and 8. For the ICTR, the territorial jurisdiction extends to the territory of Rwanda as well as to the territory of neighbouring State in respect of serious violations of international humanitarian law committed by Rwandan citizens and jurisdiction is temporally limited to the period 1 January 1994 to 31 December 1994 Statute of the ICTR Arts. 1 and 7.

[70]   M. Bassiouni, 'Historical Survey: 1919-1998', in M. Bassiouni (ed.), *ICC Ratification and National Implementing Legislation* (Toulouse, Eres 1999) 1, 24.

[71]   Statute of the ICTY Art. 9; Statute of the ICTR Art. 8.

ful enforcement mechanism. Meaningful in this context means that the Court must be capable of holding States (and more particularly, the governments within States) accountable for domestic policy choices that allow violations of human rights and humanitarian law to occur and then protect the violators from individual criminal responsibility. The complementary nature of the jurisdiction of the ICC achieves this goal in two related ways.

First, Article 17 makes States more accountable at a local level by acknowledging that States bear the primary responsibility for investigating and prosecuting allegations of crimes within the subject-matter jurisdiction of the ICC. Ostensibly this approach respects the prerogative of States under international law to exercise police power and penal law through their own systems of law enforcement and national courts, but it also has a more practical effect. When a State becomes a State Party to the Rome Statute, it is compelled, by virtue of the standard-setting role of the word 'genuinely' in Article 17, to ensure that any investigation, prosecution or decision not to prosecute involving a crime within the subject-matter jurisdiction of the ICC is carried out in a manner that complies with the minimum standard. In order for a State Party to ensure that it is capable of complying with the minimum standard, the State Party must incorporate into its domestic penal system laws that establish criminal liability at a national level for crimes within the jurisdiction of the ICC. If a State does not and a case is later referred to the ICC, the State's omission to incorporate such laws could invite the attention of the ICC and may form the foundation for a finding of unwillingness or inability.[72] States are therefore compelled, by reason of their participation in the Rome Statute, to ensure that they are capable, at a national level, of achieving at least the minimum standard of investigation and prosecution required by the Statute.

The second way in which the complementary jurisdiction of the ICC brings greater accountability to States for their domestic policy choices is through the actual operation of Article 17. If a State fails, through unwillingness or inability, to enforce, at a national level, individual criminal responsibility for a crime within the subject-matter jurisdiction of the ICC, the Court can potentially assume jurisdiction over the case. In this way, the

---

[72] See, generally, K. Doherty and T. McCormack, "Complementarity' As A Catalyst For Comprehensive Domestic Penal Legislation', 5 *UC Davis J Intl L & Policy* (1999), 152.

Court can hold the State accountable for decisions made at a local level, and again it is the standard-setting function of 'genuinely' in Article 17 that makes this possible. 'Genuinely' sets the minimum standard to which States must adhere when carrying out either an investigation or prosecution of such a case or when making a decision not to prosecute such a case. If a State is unwilling or unable to meet this minimum standard, then the door is opened for the ICC to assume jurisdiction over the case. In this instance Article 17 makes the State more accountable at an international level.

Article 17 therefore gives the ICC the ability to penetrate the shield of impunity that has often been used by States to protect the perpetrators of humanitarian and human rights law violations and provides the foundation necessary for the Court to become a truly meaningful enforcement mechanism at an international level.

3. CONCLUSION

International law has developed in a manner that has gradually placed more emphasis upon the individual as a subject of international law. In the areas of international human rights law and international humanitarian law, this has meant affording greater protection to individuals from the harm brought about by violations of these laws. One method of ensuring greater protection has been the evolution of the notion of individual criminal responsibility for violations of these laws. However, individual criminal responsibility is a hollow notion in the absence of a will actually to enforce that responsibility in the appropriate circumstances. To the extent that enforcing individual criminal responsibility for serious violations of international human rights and humanitarian law has, historically, been the sole responsibility of States, there has existed a gap between the need to hold individuals responsible for serious violations and the desire of States to bring such individuals to justice. The lack of desire on the part of States has been a consequence of domestic policy choices being informed by matters of *realpolitik* with the result that State inaction has often provided a shield to individuals committing these violations, behind which those individuals have been able to hide. Developing a meaningful enforcement mechanism capable of holding States accountable for domestic policy choices that offer impunity to violators has been an ongoing project evolving over many years and the establishment of the ICC represents a milestone in that evolution.

For the first time in history, there now exists an international enforcement mechanism that can hold States accountable, in a meaningful way, for their failure to bring the perpetrators of the most serious crimes of international concern to justice. In so doing, the ICC raises the level of individual criminal responsibility attached to the commission of these crimes because it provides a forum for ensuring that individuals who commit these crimes will actually be held responsible for them, either at a domestic or international level. Therefore, individual criminal responsibility is enforced through the ability of the ICC to hold States accountable for their domestic policy choices and a major feature of this new level of accountability is the presence of the word 'genuinely' in Article 17.

By setting a minimum standard to which States must adhere when carrying out either an investigation or prosecution of a case involving a crime within the subject-matter jurisdiction of the ICC or when making a decision whether to prosecute such a case, the word 'genuinely' provides the essential link between assigning individual criminal responsibility for these crimes and bringing about the enforcement of that responsibility in a meaningful way. In this regard, if a State is unwilling or unable to enforce individual criminal responsibility in circumstances that warrant it, the State can be held accountable for its unwillingness or inability and the accused individual can be prosecuted in an alternative international forum, namely the ICC.

Ensuring individual criminal responsibility through State accountability is a new development in the area of international criminal law, but it is one that has the potential to bridge the gap that has existed for so long between the need to hold individuals responsible for serious violations and the desire of States to bring such individuals to justice. However, it is already apparent that many States are not willing to participate in a process that might subject them to greater accountability and those States are not yet parties to the Rome Statute. Even among States that are States Parties to the Rome Statute, there is still much ground to be covered before it can be concluded that the ICC is a meaningful enforcement mechanism in a practical sense. Much will turn on the extent to which States are willing to cooperate with the Court, especially in those instances where the Court has determined that those same States have been unwilling to meet the minimum standard required by Article 17. What is required is an ongoing commitment by States to the main goal of the Rome Statute, which is to bring an end to impunity for the perpetrators of the most serious crimes of international concern to the international community as a whole. It is a lofty goal but one that is all the more achievable through the establishment of the ICC and the presence of the word 'genuinely' in Article 17.

COMMENTS ON CHAPTER 5 OF ROD JENSEN

*Bert Swart**

Rod Jensen has written an excellent chapter, which first discusses some aspects of Article 17 of the Rome Statute. He then turns towards factors that inform the need to strike a balance between the Court's effective operation, on the one hand, and the need for States to protect their sovereignty and national interests, on the other hand. With regard to the word 'genuinely' in Article 17, Rod Jensen is probably right not to worry too much about its precise meaning. When reading him, as well as other commentators on Article 17, one gets the impression that the word 'genuinely' may well be redundant. It does not seem really to affect the obligations of States nor the power of the ICC to supervise them. It rather expresses what would be obvious without the word being included in the text of Article 17.

Thus, as Rod Jensen has done in his chapter, I too would like to turn to the more fundamental issues that he has raised and make a number of comments. Rod Jensen provides an excellent analysis of a series of factors that, in the past, induced States to accept impunity. He also convincingly explains the uniqueness of the complementarity system in the ICC Statute in its attempt to bring an end to impunity. I agree to a large extent with his analysis, and I do admire its high quality. What I would like to do here is to make some comments which are meant to complement his observations. Some of my comments may also have bearing on the chapters in this book.

I have two sets of comments to make: first, some observations on the significance of human rights and human rights bodies for the work of the ICC in the sphere of complementarity; second, comments regarding the basic model underlying the Statute, which one could call a 'conflict model'.

---

* Ad Litem Judge, International Criminal Tribunal for the former Yugoslavia; Professor of International Criminal Law, University of Amsterdam.

J.K. Kleffner & G. Kor (eds.), Complementary Views on Complementarity
© 2006, T·M·C· ASSER PRESS, The Hague, The Netherlands and the Authors

Let me first turn to human rights developments. Rod Jensen rightly notes that one of the fundamental developments of the last decennia has been the recognition of the individual as a subject of international law. Nuremberg and later developments in international humanitarian law emphasize the duties of the individual under international law. Human rights treaties, on the other hand, accord him rights. The fact that the individual has been recognized as a bearer of rights in international human rights treaties is of fundamental importance to the creation of the Statute. In that respect I find myself in full agreement with Rod Jensen. I would like to add some observations, however.

Firstly, on a historical note, the case law of international human rights bodies has made an important contribution to the creation of the International Criminal Court, and, one might add, to that of the *ad hoc* tribunals. We are all familiar with the case law of the Inter-American Court of Human Rights, the Human Rights Committee, and, to a lesser extent, the European Court of Human Rights on matters of impunity. International crimes committed by State agents have been the object of scrutiny by these supervisory bodies since the beginning of the 1980s in the past century. Cases like *Velasquez Rodriguez*[1] and *Baboeram*[2] have enabled international judicial bodies themselves to pronounce on practices of impunity. I believe that this, by itself, has already contributed to the movement to create an international criminal court. In addition, there is another aspect that may have been even more important. It is the established case law of the Human Rights Committee, as well as of the Inter-American Court of Human Rights and the European Court of Human Rights, that individuals have a right under these conventions to be protected by States Parties against crimes which infringe upon their rights under the conventions, regardless of whether or not the perpetrators of these crimes are State agents and of whether or not the crimes are international crimes. Human rights conventions oblige States Parties to protect victims of crimes infringing upon their fundamental rights by preventing and repressing them to the best of their ability. One aspect of

---

[1] *Velasquez Rodriguez case (Judgment)* Inter-American Court of Human Rights Series C No. 4 (29 July 1988).

[2] *Baboeram et al.* v. *Suriname*, Communication No. 146/1983 and 148 to 154/1983 (4 April 1985) U.N. Doc. Supp. No. 40 (A/40/40) at 187 (1985).

that obligation is the duty to carry out criminal investigations and to institute criminal proceedings. A failure to do so may itself create international responsibility of the State concerned and give rise to complaints before international supervisory bodies. Ending impunity for international crimes is a matter of protecting the basic human rights of victims.

Secondly, the fact not only that those suspected or accused of crimes have rights under human rights conventions but also that the same is true for victims is not solely of historical importance for the International Criminal Court. In answering the question of whether or not a State has 'genuinely' carried out 'the investigation or prosecution', recourse may be had to the case law of international human rights bodies. In the past few years, for instance, the European Court of Human Rights has rendered a number of important judgments on the duty of States Parties to carry out criminal investigations. One gets the impression that the standards applied by the Court have gradually become more exacting and the requirements States have to satisfy in this field stricter. Good examples of the kind of criteria developed by the European Court of Human Rights in recent years are the two recent judgments in the cases of *Nachova and others* v. *Bulgaria*, decided on 26 February 2004, and *Slimani* v. *France*, decided on 27 July 2004. For instance, in the first of these cases, which is concerned with the killing of two gypsies during their arrest by the police, the European Court lays bare a whole catalogue of mistakes and other failures in the criminal investigation into the event by the Bulgarian authorities.

Thirdly, what are the consequences of a finding that a State failed to fulfil its obligation under a human rights convention to investigate a crime properly? Under the ICC Statute the consequence would be that the International Criminal Court would take over and do what national authorities had failed to do. Under human rights conventions, however, the situation is different. The first obvious consequence is that the victim enjoys a right to compensation under an international convention itself and perhaps also under domestic law. But the more interesting and important question is whether or not international human rights bodies may order a State Party to conduct an investigation which it failed to carry out in the past or to reopen an investigation that was conducted in a totally unsatisfactory manner. It is far from sure whether the existing human rights bodies possess that power, although there are several decisions in which they have suggested or pressed States to follow this course of action. Whatever might be the case, the 'message' of a finding that a State has failed to live up to its obligations under a human rights treaty is for that State to do what is had failed to do so far: to start investigating and adjudicating the case or to try harder and to increase its efforts to bring the alleged or potential perpetrator to justice. In other words, such a finding of a human rights body offers the State the opportunity for a fresh start. A finding of unwillingness or inability by the ICC, on the other hand, does not seem to entail the possibility for a State to start again with an investigation into specific events. The Rome Statute does not provide national criminal jurisdictions with the possibility of starting an investigation or to reopen the case after a finding of unwillingness or inability, at least not explicitly and unambiguously. In other words, the ICC Statute has only one mode of responding to impunity while there may be alternatives. However, one cannot exclude the possibility that, within the framework of admissibility proceedings, the International Criminal Court may actually press a State to start or to reopen an investigation.

Let me end by making some comments on the 'conflict model' of the Statute. Rod Jensen wrote about a balance between State sovereignty and the need to penetrate the shield of impunity. That is a striking way of putting the problem of impunity in terms of a conflict model. One wonders whether there may be situations in which this model is not adequate. Two examples might illustrate the point.

First, there may be situations in which a State is clearly not able to prosecute certain offences, recognizes its own inability, and prefers to refer the case to the ICC. In this situation an easy and effective solution would be for that State to enter into negotiations with the Prosecutor in The Hague and to invite him to take over the case at hand. In the structure of the ICC Statute, this is somewhat complicated. One first has to pass the admissibility stage in which the Court has to make a finding of unwillingness or inability, a finding which implies a shortcoming of that State and which officially declares that it is not able to fulfil its obligations. In other words, the whole cumbersome machinery of complementarity proceedings has to be followed in order to find a solution for something that might already be quite obvious. This machinery is unnecessary in such cases and one could choose a more effective and time saving way of coming to a solution.

Secondly, with regard to cases in which States appear to be unwilling to investigate or prosecute, one has to realize that this category may cover rather diverse situations. There may, for instance, be the situation in which a State itself is unwilling to investigate or prosecute a case because the political situation does not permit it to do so while it would not object to the ICC handling the case. Here again one would have to go through the whole machinery of complementarity proceedings. An official declaration that a State is unwilling would be required. However, the State itself is only unwilling to investigate or prosecute the case but not to have it prosecuted by the ICC.

In sum, the conflict model of the ICC Statute may not cover all the situations in which there might be a legitimate need for the ICC to intervene. One therefore wonders whether it would not have been advisable to think about the relationship between the ICC and national criminal jurisdictions in a more open, less antagonistic way. In his chapter, Rod Jensen refers to the concept of global governance. That concept, however, enables us also to reflect on the most rational solutions, which, by including the notion of cooperation, do not always coincide necessarily with the conflict model of the Statute.

INDEX